*Python Machine Learning Illustrated Guide For Beginners & Intermediates*

© **Healthy Pragmatic Solutions Inc. Copyright 2017 - All rights reserved.**

The contents of this book may not be reproduced, duplicated or transmitted without direct written permission from the author.

Under no circumstances will any legal responsibility or blame be held against the publisher for any reparation, damages, or monetary loss due to the information herein, either directly or indirectly.

**Legal Notice:**

You cannot amend, distribute, sell, use, quote or paraphrase any part or the content within this book without the consent of the author.

**Disclaimer Notice:**

Please note the information contained within this document is for educational purposes only. No warranties of any kind are expressed or implied. Readers acknowledge that the author is not engaging in the rendering of legal, financial, medical or professional advice. Please consult a licensed professional before attempting any techniques outlined in this book.

By reading this document, the reader agrees that under no circumstances are is the author responsible for any losses, direct or indirect, which are incurred as a result of the use of information contained within this document, including, but not limited to, — errors, omissions, or inaccuracies.

# Contents

Introduction .......................................... 12

Chapter 1 ............................................. 14

Introduction to machine Learning .................. 14

    Definition ...................................... 14

    How Machines Learn? ........................... 15

    Importance of Machine Learning ............. 17

    Types of Machine Learning .................... 19

    Conclusion ...................................... 22

Chapter 2 ............................................. 24

  Environment Setup ............................... 24

    Downloading and Installing Anaconda .... 25

    Running your First Program ................... 33

Chapter 3 ............................................. 43

  Data Preprocessing For Machine Learning .. 43

    Getting the Dataset ............................ 44

    Import Libraries ................................. 46

    Import the Dataset ............................. 48

    Handling Missing Values ...................... 53

    Handling Categorical Data .................... 56

    Dividing data into training and tests sets. 58

Scaling the Data ........................................60

Chapter 4..........................................................64

  Linear Regression..........................................64

    Theory of Linear Regression......................64

    Linear Regression with One Variable ........67

    Linear Regression with Multiple Variables ...............................................................78

Chapter 5..........................................................88

  Polynomial Regression..................................88

  Polynomial Regression with Python Scikit Learn ............................................................91

Chapter 6........................................................102

    Decision Tree for Regression ..................102

    Benefits of Decision Trees.......................106

    Using Python Scikit Learn Library to Implement Decision Trees ......................107

Chapter 7........................................................115

  Random Forest for Regression....................115

    Working of Random Forest Algorithm ...116

    Pros of Random Forest Algorithm..........117

    Cons of Random Forest Algorithm.........118

Implementing Random Forest Algorithm using Scikit Learn ................................... 119

## Chapter 8 ........................................ 127

Support Vector Regression ....................... 127

SVM Theory .......................................... 128

## Chapter 9 ........................................ 139

Naïve Bayes Algorithm for Classification ... 139

Theory of Naïve Bayes (NB) Algorithm .. 140

Advantages of Naïve Bayes Algorithm ... 145

Disadvantages of Naïve Bayes Algorithm ............................................................. 145

Naïve Bayes Algorithm Applications ...... 146

Implementing Naïve Bayes Algorithm With Python Scikit Learn ................................. 147

## Chapter 10 ..................................... 159

K Nearest Neighbors Algorithm for Classification ............................................. 159

Theory of KNN ....................................... 159

Advantages of KNN Algorithm ............... 162

Disadvantages of KNN Algorithm ........... 163

KNN Implementation with Scikit Learn .. 163

Effect of Value of K on Prediction Accuracy ............................................................. 171

Chapter 11 ...................................................... 174

  Decision Tree for Classification ................... 174

    Solving Classification Problems with Decision Tree in Python Scikit Learn ....... 175

Chapter 12 ...................................................... 183

  Random Forest for Classification ................ 183

    Implementing Random Forest Classification with Python's Scikit Learn ...................... 184

Chapter 13 ...................................................... 192

  Support Vector Machines for Classification ............................................................. 192

    SVM for classification using Python's Scikit Learn ...................................................... 193

Chapter 14 ...................................................... 201

  K Means Clustering Algorithm .................... 201

    Steps of K-Mean Clustering ..................... 201

Chapter 15 ...................................................... 211

  Hierarchical Clustering ............................... 211

    Hierarchical Clustering Theory ............... 212

Hierarchical Clustering with Python Scikit Learn ....................................................... 220

## Chapter 16 .................................................... 226

Dimensionality Reduction with PCA .......... 226

Principal Component Analysis Theory ... 227

Implementing PCA with Sklearn ............ 229

## Chapter 17 .................................................... 239

Dimensionality Reduction with LDA .......... 239

Linear Discriminant Analysis Theory ...... 240

Implementing LDA with Scikit Learn ...... 240

## Chapter 18 .................................................... 248

Performance Evaluation with Cross Validation and Grid Search .......................................... 248

Cross Validation ..................................... 249

Cross Validation with Python's Scikit Learn ............................................................... 250

Gird Search for Parameter Selection ..... 256

Implementing Grid Search with Sklearn 257

*You Might Also Be Interested In...*

**Book Link:** *https://amzn.to/2AiwYHf*

***FREE E-BOOK DOWNLOAD :***

**http://bit.ly/2yJsyq4**

**or**

**http://pragmaticsolutionstech.com/**

Use the link above to get instant access to the bestselling E-Book **Data Analytics' Guide For Beginners**

# ***RESOURCES:***

All the datasets that we are going to use in this book can be found at this link:

https://drive.google.com/file/d/1TB0tMuLvuL0Ad1dzHRyxBX9cseOhUs_4/view?usp=sharing

*Also, you can find all scripts used in the book within this link below:*

https://drive.google.com/file/d/1qn9G-W7v2mXcTSxk9ejbqiHjD_pxat1U/view?usp=sharing

## *Introduction*

Machine learning is one of the hottest buzz words around. With the advancement in high computing hardware and availability of thousands of terra bytes of data, more and more companies and research organizations are using machine learning to build intelligent machines that can perform variety of tasks and can help humans make better decisions.

This book contains detailed overview of all the latest concepts in machine learning. Each chapter in this book is dedicated to one machine learning algorithm. Each chapter begins with the brief theory of the algorithm followed by implementation of the algorithm in Python's Scikit learn library.

The book is aimed towards novice as well as expert users. On hand it can be used as handbook of machine learning for the beginners, while on the other hand it can also be used by expert users as reference for different machine learning algorithms. To get out of this book, you are requested to not mere read the book but to actually hand code all the examples provided in this book.

In the end, I wish you best in your machine learning endeavors. I hope once you read this book, you have all the basic tools in your machine learning arsenal to solve any type of machine learning problem.

## Chapter 1

## Introduction to machine Learning

Machine learning is a branch of Artificial Intelligence that deals with learning implicitly from data using various statistical techniques. Unlike traditional computer programs where all the application logic is explicitly programed, machine learning applications learn implicitly from the data without being explicitly programmed. The idea behind machine learning is that instead of hard coded logic, large amount of data is fed into the application. It is then the responsibility of the application to learn from that data and make decisions.

### Definition

The first definition of machine learning was coined by Arthur Samuel back in 1959. He defined machine learning as:

*"Field of study that enables computers to learn without being explicitly programmed."*

Tom Mitchel from Carnegie Mellon University defined machine learning in mathematically understandable terms as in 1997. He said:

*"A computer program is said to learn from experience E with respect to some task T and some performance measure P, if its performance on T, as measured by P, improves with experience E."*

The definition provided by Tom Mitchel is widely regarded as the most precise yet clear definition of machine learning. Now we know what machine learning is, but a question still remains that how machines learning and what is their inner working. The next section will answer this question:

### *How Machines Learn?*

Before dwelling into the details of machine learning, let us first recapitulate that how humans learn. For instance, how we humans know that we should not touch a heating plates when they are on with bare hands. How we know that they can cause burns? Well there can be two possibilities: Either we have been burned in the past by heating stove or we have been taught by elders not to touch the heating plates. In both the cases we have had some experience in the past that stops us from touching heating plates when they are on. In other words, we had some past information, on the basis of which we make future decisions.

Machine learns in a similar way. In the beginning they have no knowledge. They are just like a newborn child with zero knowledge. To make machines learn, information is passed to these machines. From this information, machines identify patterns using various statistical techniques. Once machines learn to identify patterns from the data for making decisions, they can be used to make decisions on unseen data.

Workflow of a typical learning process of a machine learning model is shown in the following figure:

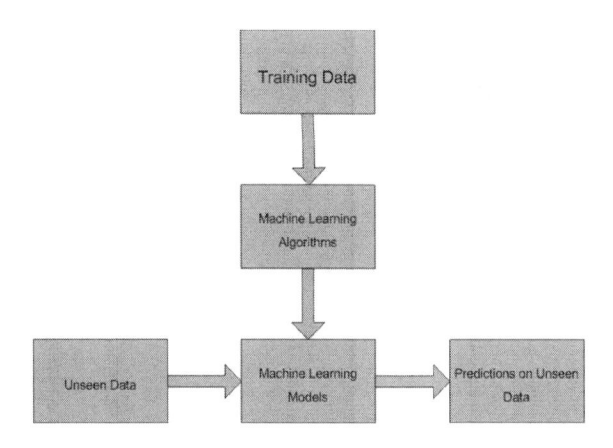

Training data is fed into machine learning algorithms that are nothing but complex mathematical algorithms. The algorithms results in machine learning models. Machine learning models are capable of making predictions on new unseen data which is also known as test data.

## *Importance of Machine Learning*

The ultimate goal of AI is to make machines as intelligent as humans. However initial work in AI showed that we cannot hardcode machines that are as intelligent as humans. Humans learn from the environment which is consistently evolving. Therefore, the best way to make intelligent machines is to make them learn themselves. Therefore, machine learning was recognized as a discipline of science that teaches machines how to automatically learn from the data.

The idea behind machine learning is that instead of hardcoding the logic, data is fed into the machines and make machines themselves learn from the data by identifying patterns from the data. Interestingly machines learning techniques are quicker than humans in identifying patterns.

Machine learning techniques have been around for quite a while. However owing to the lack of high performance hardware, these techniques were not implemented before to solve real world problems. Now, with the availability of complex hardware and huge amount of data, machine learning techniques have resurfaced and have been successful in developing intelligent machines.

## *Types of Machine Learning*

Machine learning techniques have been broadly categorized into two types:

1- Supervised Learning
2- Unsupervised Learning

### *1. Supervised Learning*

In supervised learning, both the input data and the corresponding category that the input data belongs to is provided to the learning algorithm. The learning algorithm learns the relationship between the input and the output and then predicts the output of the unseen input data samples.

For instance, supervised machine learning algorithm is fed with images of apples labeled as fruit and potatoes labeled as vegetable. After training on this data, the supervised machine learning algorithm should be able to classify new unlabeled images of apples as fruit and unlabeled potatoes as vegetable.

Following are the steps involved in supervised machine learning algorithm:

1- Feed the algorithm with input records X, and output labels y.
2- For each input record the algorithm predicts an output y'.
3- Error in prediction is calculated by subtracting y from y'.
4- The algorithm corrects itself by removing the error.
5- Steps 1 to 4 continue for multiple iterations until error is minimized.

In mathematical terms, you have input variable X and output variable y, and you have to find a function that captures relationship between the two i.e.

$$y= f(X)$$

Supervised Learning is used to solve two different types of problems: classification and regression.

**Classification:** Classification refers to process of predicting discrete output values for an input. For instance, given an input predicting whether a mail is spam or ham, a tumor is benign or malignant or whether a student will pass or fail the exam.

**Regression:** In regression problems the task of machine learning model is to predict a continuous value. For instance for given input, predict the price of the house or predict the marks obtained by a student on an exam e.tc.

### 2. *Unsupervised Learning*

In supervised learning, the algorithms are fed with the input data with no labels. It is the responsibility of the algorithm to identify patterns in the data and cluster records with similar characteristics. Normally, most of the real world data is unlabeled; therefore unsupervised learning can be used as a precursor to supervised learning.

For instance, customers shopping trend can be fed into an unsupervised learning algorithm. The algorithm can find trends in the shopping. Consider a scenario where the algorithm finds that the customers who buy baby products also buy milk. Therefore, a business decision to place the milk close to the baby products can be based on this information.

### *Conclusion*

In this chapter we introduced the machine learning as subject matter. We saw what machine learning is and what different types of machine learning are. The next chapter is dedicated to installing the software required to run machine learning algorithms in this chapter. We will be using Python's Scikit Learn Library for implementing different machine learning algorithms.

## Chapter 2

## Environment Setup

In this chapter we will install the software that we are going to use to run our Machine learning Programs. There are several options available to implement machine learning, however we will be using Python since most of the advanced machine learning community is working with Python for machine learning. To install Python several options available. You can simply install core Python and use a text editor like notepad to write Python programs. These programs can then be run via command line utilities. The other option is to install an Integrated Develop Environment (IDE) for Python. IDE provides a complete programming environment including Python installation, Editors and debugging tools. Most of the advanced programmers take the IDE route for Python development. We are also going to take the same route.

Anaconda is the IDE that we are going to use throughout this book. Anaconda is light, easy to install and comes with variety of development tools. Anaconda has its own command line utility to install third party software. And the good thing is that with Anaconda, you don't have to separately install Python environment.

## *Downloading and Installing Anaconda*

Follow these steps to download and install anaconda. In this section we will show the process of installing Anaconda for windows. The installation process remains almost same for Linux and Mac.

1- Go to the following URL https://www.anaconda.com/download/
2- You will be presented with the following webpage. Select Python 3.6 version as this is currently the latest version of Python. Click the "Download" button to download the

executable file. It takes 2-3 minutes to download the file depending upon the speed of your internet.

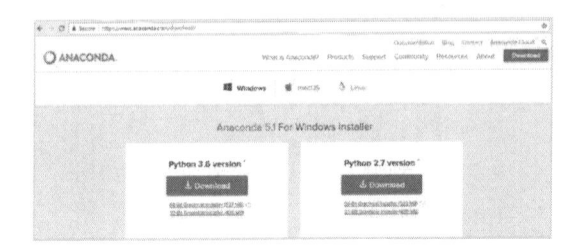

3- Once the executable file is downloaded, go to the download folder and run the executable. The name of the executable file should be similar to "Anaconda3-5.1.0-Windows-x86_64." When you run the file you will see installation wizard like the one in the following screenshot. Click "Next" button.

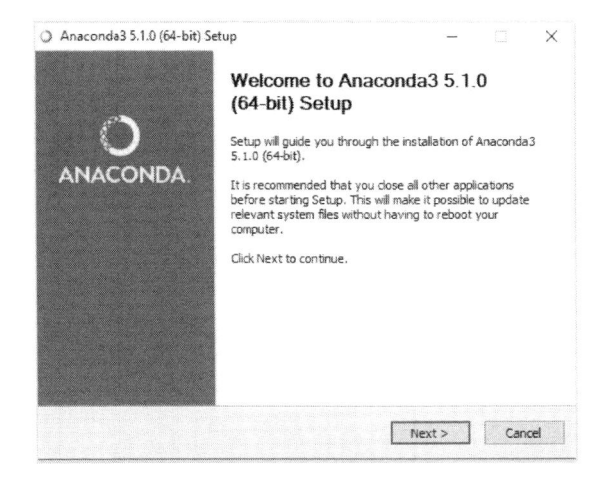

4- "License Agreement" dialogue box will appear. Read the license agreement and Click "I Agree" button.

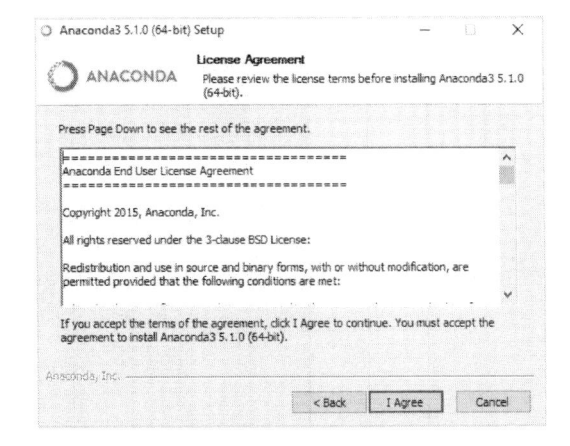

5- From the "Select Installation Type" dialogue box, check the "Just Me" radio button and click "Next" button as shown in the following screenshot.

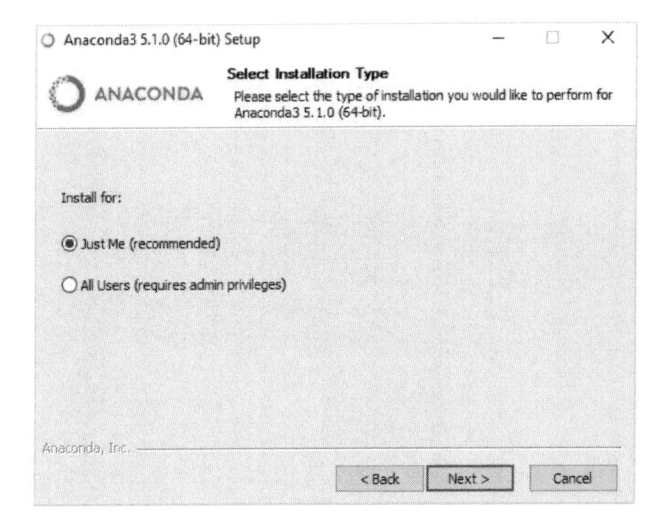

6- Choose the installation directory (Default is preferred) from the "Choose Install Location" dialogue box and click "Next" button. You should have around 3 GB of free space in your installation directory.

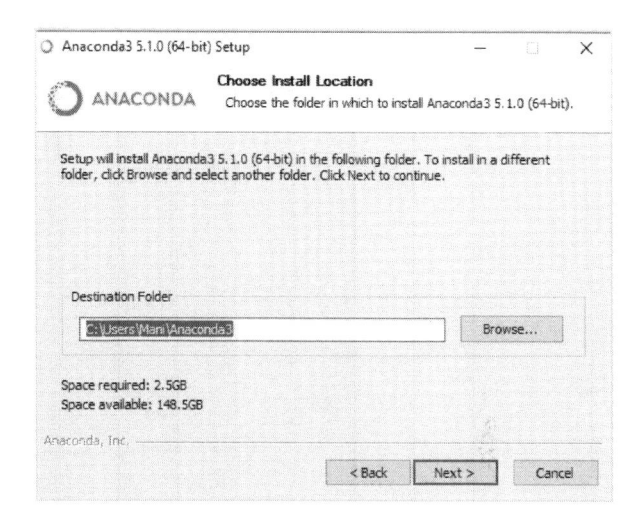

7- From the "Advanced Installation Options" dialogue box, select the second checkbox "Register Anaconda as my default Python 3.6" and click the "Install" button as shown in the following screenshot.

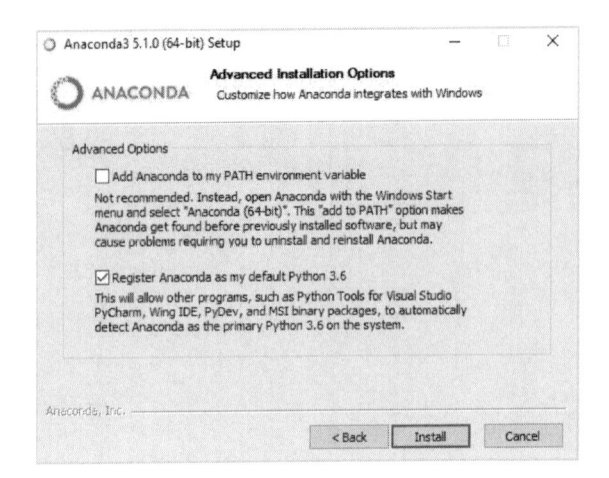

The installation process will start which can take some time to complete. Sit back and enjoy a cup of coffee.

8- Once the installation completes, click the "Next" button as shown below.

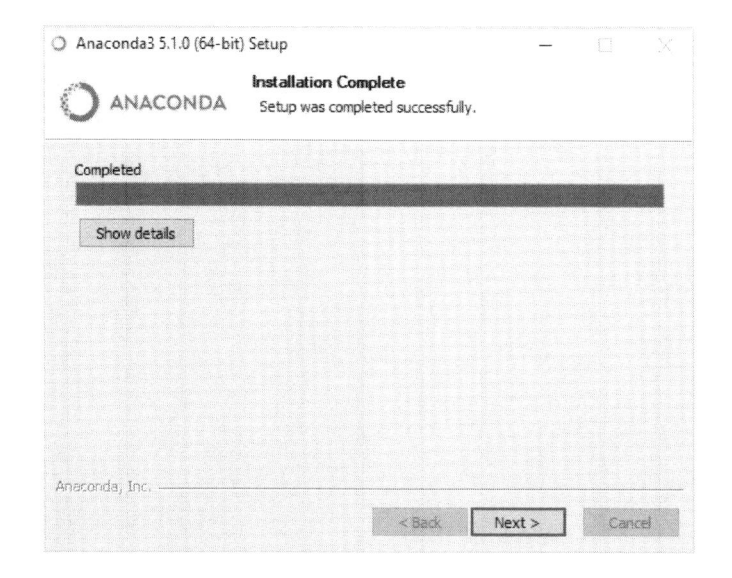

9- "Microsoft Visual Studio Code Installation" window appear, click "Skip" button.

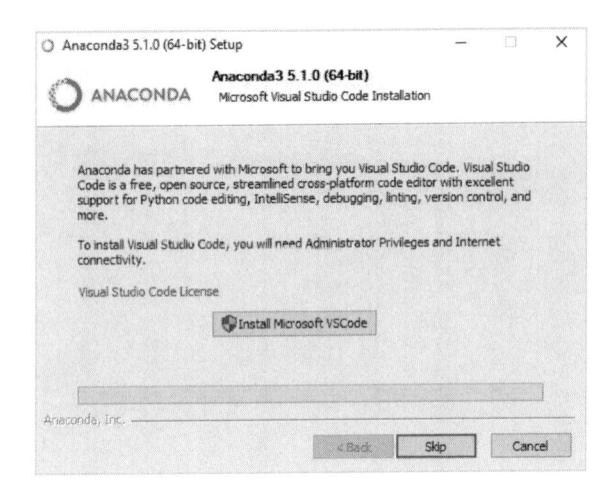

10- Congratulations, you have installed Anaconda. Uncheck the both the checkboxes on the dialogue box that appears and "Finish" button.

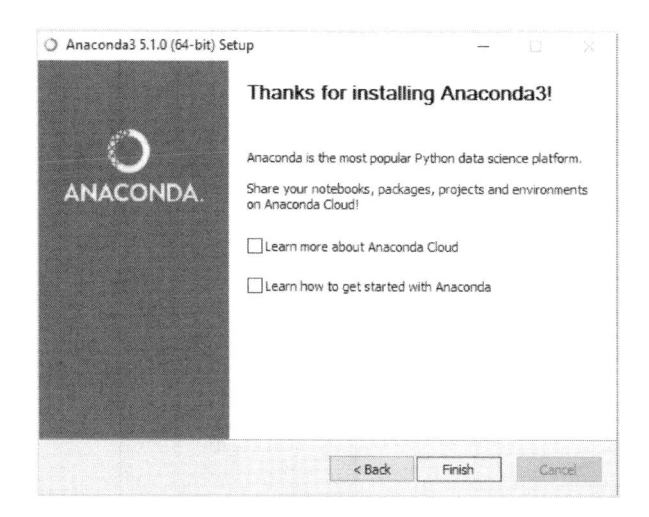

## *Running your First Program*

We have installed environment required to run Python scripts. Now is the time to run our first program. With Anaconda, you have several ways to do so. We will see two of those in this section.

Go to your window search box and type "Anaconda Navigator" and then select the "Anaconda Navigator" application as shown below:

**Anaconda Navigator**
Desktop app

**Folders**

- anaconda_navigator - in site-packages
- anaconda_navigator - in site-packages
- anaconda_navigator-1.7.0-py3.6.egg-info - in site-packages
- anaconda_navigator-1.7.0-py3.6.egg-info - in site-packages
- anaconda-navigator-1.7.0-py36_0

**Search suggestions**

- Anaconda Navigator - See web results
- anaconda navigator **youtube**
- anaconda navigator **windows**
- anaconda navigator **download**
- anaconda navigator **app**

Anaconda Navigator

Anaconda Navigator Dashboard will appear that looks like this.

Note: It takes some time for Anaconda Navigator to start, so be patient.

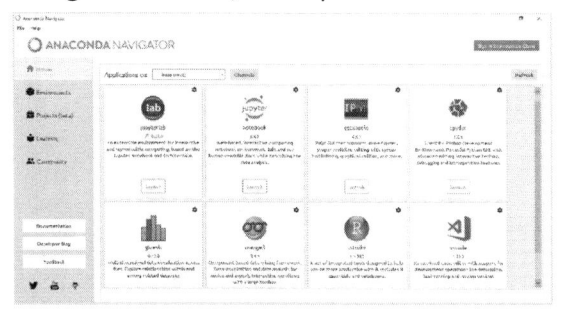

From the dashboard, you can see all of the tools available to develop your python applications. In this book we will mostly use "Jupyter Notebook" (second from top). Though in this chapter we shall also see how to run python script via "Spyder".

**Running Scripts via Jupyter Notebook**

Jupyter notebook runs in your default browser. From the navigator, launch "Jupyter Notebook" (Second option from the top).

Another way to launch Jupyter is by typing "Jupyter Notebook" in the search box and selecting the "Jupyter Notebook" application from the start menu as shown below:

**Jupyter Notebook**
Desktop app

**Folders**

jupyter_notebook_config.d - in jupyter

jupyter_notebook_config.d - in jupyter

**Documents**

jupyter-notebook-script

jupyter_notebook_config

**Search suggestions**

jupyter notebook - See web results

jupyter notebook download

jupyter notebook login

jupyter notebook online

jupyter notebook app

jupyter notebook images

jupyter notebook

Jupyter notebook will launch in a new tab of your default browser.

To create a new notebook, click "new" button at the top-right corner of the Jupyter notebook dashboard. From dropdown, select "Python 3."

You will see new Python 3 notebook that looks like this:

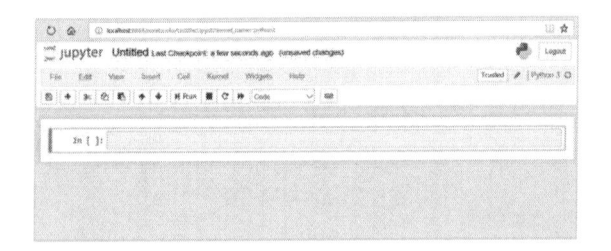

Jupyter notebook consists of cells. Python script is written inside these cells. Let's print hello world using Jupyter notebook. In the first cell of the notebook enter "print('hello world') and press CTRL+ ENTER. The script in the first cell will be executed as shown below:

The "print" function prints the string passed to it as parameter, in the output. To create a new cell, click the "+" button from the top left menu as shown below:

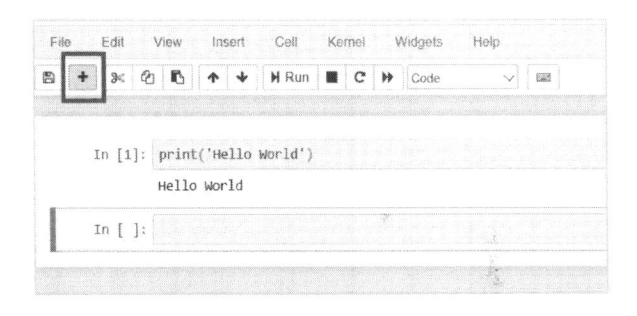

You can write Python script in the new cell and press CTRL + ENTER to execute it.

## Running Scripts via Spyder

While Jupyter notebook is a good place to start writing Python programs, once you get comfortable with Python, you should move to Spyder IDE. Spyder allows us to directly create Python files. Spyder is similar to more conventional text editors with options to Run file, Run piece of code, debug code etc.

Just like Jupyter notebook, you can run Spyder from Anaconda Navigator or directly from Start Menu. You will be presented with the following interface once you run Spyder.

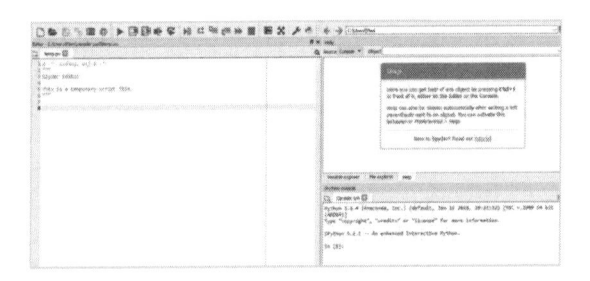

On the left side of the Spyder interface, you can see text editor; this is where you enter your script. On the bottom right you have console window. You can directly execute scripts in the console window. Furthermore, the output of the code written in the editor also appears in the console window. Let's write hello world program in Spyder.

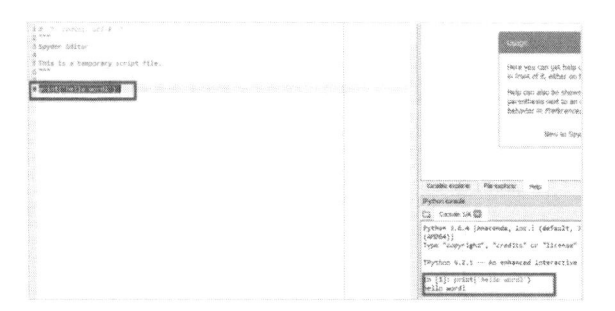

To run script in Python you have two options. You can either click the green triangle from the top menu or you can select the piece of code you want to execute and press CTRL + ENTER from the keyboard. You will see the output in the console window.

**What's next?**

In this chapter we saw the process of setting up the environment required to run python programs. We wrote our first python program in two different editors. In the next chapter we will start our discussion about data preprocessing for machine learning.

## Chapter 3

## Data Preprocessing For Machine Learning

Data has to be in a specific format before you can apply machine learning algorithms to them. Converting data to the right format for machine learning algorithms is usually known as data preprocessing. Depending upon the dataset, there are several preprocessing steps that are required to be performed to convert data into a format usable by machine learning algorithm. Following are the steps involved in preprocessing data for machine learning algorithms:

1- Getting the dataset
2- Import libraries
3- Import the dataset
4- Handling missing values

5- Handling categorical data
6- Dividing data into training and tests sets
7- Scaling the data

In this chapter we will study each of these steps in details.

## *Getting the Dataset*

All the datasets that we are going to use in this book can be found at this link:

https://drive.google.com/file/d/1TB0tMuLvuL0Ad1dzHRyxBX9cseOhUs_4/view?usp=sharing

Download the "rar" file, and copy the "Datasets" folder into your D drive. All the algorithms in the book access the datasets from "D:/Datasets" folder. The dataset that we are going to use in this first chapter for preprocessing is called "patients.csv".

If you go to your Datasets folder and open the patients.csv file with Microsoft Excel, it looks like this:

| Age | BMI | Gender | Diabetic |
|---|---|---|---|
| 25 | 25 | Male | No |
| 55 | 31 | Female | Yes |
| 40 | 28 | Male | Yes |
| 61 | 24 | Male | No |
| 24 |  | Female | No |
| 35 | 35 | Male | Yes |
| 52 | 32 | Male | Yes |
| 67 | 26 | Female | No |
| 44 | 27 | Male | No |
| 19 | 22 | Female | No |
| 58 | 89 | Female | Yes |
| 48 | 39 | Male | Yes |

The dataset contains information about Age, BMI (Body Mass Index) and Gender of 12 patients. The dataset also contains a column that shows whether patients are Diabetic or not. The Age and BMI columns are numeric since they contain numeric values while the Gender and Diabetic columns are categorical.

Another important distinction that you need to make before you use your dataset for machine learning is between independent and dependent variable. As a rule of thumb, the variable whose value is to be predicted is dependent variable and the variables that are used for making predictions are independent variables. For instance in the patients.csv dataset, Age, BMI and Gender variables are independent while the fourth column i.e. Diabetic is the dependent variable as its value is dependent on the first three columns.

## *Import Libraries*

Python comes with a variety of prebuild libraries that perform different tasks. In this book we will be using Python's Scikit Learn Library. However for now we will only install three of the most essential libraries that we will need in almost every machine learning application. These libraries are *numpy*, *matplotlib.pyplot* and *pandas*.

### *numpy*

The *numpy* library is used performs variety of advanced mathematical functions. Since machine learning algorithms make heavy use of mathematics, it is highly recommended that you install the *numpy* library.

### *matplotlib.pyplot*

This library is used to plot beautiful charts. To get intuition about our data and results, we will need to this library.

### *pandas*

Finally, the third library that we are going to install in this chapter is the *pandas* library. The *pandas* library is used to easily import and view the datasets.

To import these three libraries, create a new Python notebook in *Jupyter* or Open a new file in *Spyder* (The codes in this chapter are executed in *Spyder*) and execute the following lines of code.

```
import numpy as np
import matplotlib.pyplot as plt
import pandas as pd
```

To import a library in Python, keyword *import* is used. In the script above we import *numpy* as *np, matplotlib.pyplot* as *plt* and *pandas* as *pd*, respectively. Here *np, plt* and *pd* are nicknames. We will use these nicknames to call different functions of these libraries.

## *Import the Dataset*

We have downloaded the libraries in last section. In this section, we will import the dataset into the application that we created in last section. You will also get to know why we imported the *pandas* library.

Our dataset is in CSV (Comma Separated Values) format. The *pandas* library contains *read_csv* function that takes the path to the CSV formatted dataset as parameter and loads the dataset into *pandas dataframe* which is basically an object that stores dataset in the form of columns and rows.

Execute the following script (below the script that loads the libraries) to load the patients.csv dataset to the application.

```
patient_data =
pd.read_csv("D:/Datasets/patients.csv")
```

The script above loads the patients.csv dataset in the Datasets folder of the D drive to **patients_data dataframe.**

If you are using *Jupyter* notebook, simply execute the following script to see how your data looks:

```
patient_data.head()
```

On the other hand, if you are using *Spyder*, go to Variable explorer and double click *patient_data* variable from the list of variables as shown below:

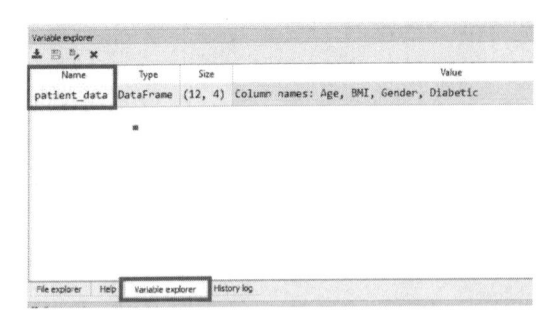

Once you click the *patient_data* variable, you will see the details of the patients.csv dataset as shown in the figure below:

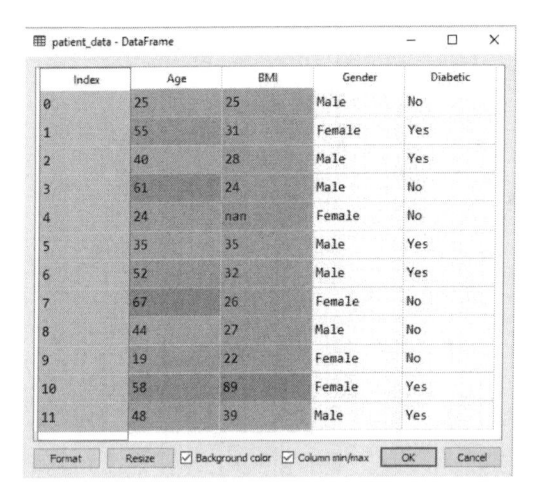

You can see that a *pandas dataframe* looks like a matrix with zero based index.

Once we have loaded the dataset, the next step is to divide the dataset into a matrix of features and vector of dependent variables. Feature set consists of all the independent variables. For instance the feature matrix for the patients.csv dataset will contain Age, BMI and Gender columns. The size of the feature matrix is equal to the number of independent variables by the number of records. In this case the feature matrix will be of size 3 x 12 since there are three independent variable and 12 records.

Let's first create a feature features. You can give any name to the feature matrix but conventionally in machine learning community, feature matrix is denoted by capital X. However for the sake of readability we will name it *features* Execute the following script:

```
features= patient_data.iloc[:,0:3].values
```

In the script above we use the *iloc* function of the *dataframe* to select all the rows and the first three columns from the *patient_data* dataframe. The iloc function takes two parameters. The first is the range of rows to select and the second is the range of columns to select. We only specified colon as first parameter which means that filter all the rows from the dataset. In the second parameter after the comma we specified a range of columns i.e. column 0 to 3. This returns columns 0, 1 and 2. Remember the *iloc* returns one less than the upper range of column. The 0, 1 and 2 columns mean Age, BMI and Gender since python follows zero based index. Therefore Age is considered $0^{th}$ column.

If now you print the features in the console window, you will see following result:

```
array([[25, 25.0, 'Male'],
       [55, 31.0, 'Female'],
       [40, 28.0, 'Male'],
       [61, 24.0, 'Male'],
       [24, nan, 'Female'],
       [35, 35.0, 'Male'],
       [52, 32.0, 'Male'],
       [67, 26.0, 'Female'],
       [44, 27.0, 'Male'],
       [19, 22.0, 'Female'],
       [58, 89.0, 'Female'],
       [48, 39.0, 'Male']], dtype=object)
```

You can see it is a two dimensional array of feature set.

Similarly, to create a label vector, execute the following script:

```
labels= patient_data.iloc[:,3].values
```

Now we have our feature matrix as well as label vector. The next step is to handle the missing values (if any) in the dataset.

### Handling Missing Values

If you look at the patient_data object you will see that the record at index 4 has missing value for BMI column. To handle missing values, the simplest approach is to remove the record with missing values. However, sometimes a record contains crucial information and should not be removed just because one column has a missing value.

Another approach to deal with missing values is to replace missing value with some value. Missing values can be replaced by mean or median of all the values in the column.

To handle the missing values we will use the *Imputer* class of the *sklearn.preprocessing* library. Take a look at the following script.

```
from      sklearn.preprocessing import Imputer
imputer                         = Imputer(missing_values="NaN", strategy="mean", axis=0)
imputer                         = imputer.fit(features[:,1:2])
features[:,1:2]                 = imputer.transform(features[:,1:2])
```

In the script above, the first line imports the *Imputer* class from *sklearn.preprocessing* library. Next we create object of the Imputer class. Imputer class constructor takes three parameters: *missing_value*, *strategy* and *axis*. The missing_value parameter specifies the value that is required to be replaced. In our dataset, missing values have been denoted by "nan", therefore we specified "NaN" for *missing_value* parameter. Strategy parameter specifies the type of strategy we want to use to fill missing value, it can have *mean, median*, and *most_frequent* values. Finally, the *axis* parameter denotes the axis along which we want to imputate. The *axis 0* specifies the column axis whereas *axis 1* specifies the row axis.

Next we execute *fit* method of the Imputer class. This method takes the column that we want to handle missing values for, as input. Finally we execute *transform* function which actually fills missing values in column 1 by the mean of the column. When you execute the script above you will see that

that the record at index 4 that previously had missing value for column1 i.e. BMI, now contains the mean of all the values in the BMI column. This is shown in the following screenshot:

```
array([[25, 25.0, 'Male'],
       [55, 31.0, 'Female'],
       [40, 28.0, 'Male'],
       [61, 24.0, 'Male'],
       [24, 34.36363636363637, 'Female'],
       [35, 35.0, 'Male'],
       [52, 32.0, 'Male'],
       [67, 26.0, 'Female'],
       [44, 27.0, 'Male'],
       [19, 22.0, 'Female'],
       [58, 89.0, 'Female'],
       [48, 39.0, 'Male']], dtype=object)
```

## *Handling Categorical Data*

We know machine learning algorithms are based on mathematical concepts and mathematics is all about numbers. Therefore, it is convenient to convert all the categorical values in our dataset to numeric values. If we look at the patients.csv we have two columns with categorical values: Gender and Diabetic.

Luckily, in sklearn.preprocessing library we have LabelEncoder class which takes categorical column as input and returns corresponding numerical output. Take a look at the following script:

```
from     sklearn.preprocessing import LabelEncoder
labelencoder_features    = LabelEncoder()
features[:,2]= labelencoder_features.fit_transform(features[:,2])
```

Like Imputer class, *LabelEncoder* class has *fit_transform* method, which is basically a combination of *fit* and *transform* methods. The class takes categorical column as input and returns corresponding numeric values. In the script above we pass it Gender column i.e. the column at index 2 to the *LabelEncoder* class. After executing the script above if you check the values of Gender column, you will see ones and zeros in place of Male and Female as shown below:

```
array([[25, 25.0, 1],
       [55, 31.0, 0],
       [40, 28.0, 1],
       [61, 24.0, 1],
       [24, 34.36363636363637, 0],
       [35, 35.0, 1],
       [52, 32.0, 1],
       [67, 26.0, 0],
       [44, 27.0, 1],
       [19, 22.0, 0],
       [58, 89.0, 0],
       [48, 39.0, 1]], dtype=object)
```

Similarly, the labels vector can also be converted into set of numeric values as follows:

```
labels = labelencoder_features.fit_transform(labels)
```

## *Dividing data into training and tests sets*

In the first chapter we discussed that machine learning models are trained on subset of dataset and tested on another subset of the dataset. This splitting between the training and test set is done to ensure that our machine learning algorithm doesn't *overfit*. *Overfitting* refers to the phenomena where machine learning performs excellent results on training data but poor results on test data. A good machine learning model is the one that gives good result on both training and test data. That way we can say that our model has correctly learned the underlying assumptions from the dataset and can be used to correctly make decisions on any new dataset.

The *sklearn.model_selection* library contains *train_test_split* class that can be used to divide data into train and test sets. The class accepts features, labels and *test_size* as parameters. The *test_size* defines the size of the test set. Test size of 0.5 means split the data into 50% of test size and 50% of training size. The following script divides the data into 75% train size and 25% test size.

```
from sklearn.model_selection import train_test_split
train_features, test_features, train_labels, test_labels = train_test_split(features, labels, test_size = 0.25, random_state = 0)
```

When you execute the above script you will see that *train_features* variable will contain matrix of 9 features (75% of 12) while *train_labels* will contain corresponding 9 labels. Similarly *test_features* will contain a matrix of 3 features (25% of 12) while *test_labels* will contain corresponding 3 labels.

## *Scaling the Data*

The final preprocessing step before we can feed our data to machine learning algorithm is that of feature scaling. We need to scale features because in some datasets there is a huge difference between the values of different features. For instance if we add number of red blood cells of patients out patients.csv dataset, the column will have values in hundreds of thousands, on the other hand the Age column can have very small values. Many of the machines learning models use Euclidean distance to find distance between data points. If features are not scaled, these algorithms can be biased towards features with large values.

There are two ways to scale features:

Standardization: $\dfrac{x - mean(x)}{standard deviation(x)}$

And

Normalization: $\dfrac{x - min(x)}{max(x) - min(x)}$

The *sklearn.preprocessing* library contains *StandardScaler* class that can be used to implement standardization of features. Like other preprocessing classes, it contains *fit_transform* method that takes dataset as input and returns scaled dataset. The following script scales both the *train_features* and *test_features* datasets.

```
from sklearn.preprocessing import StandardScaler
feature_scaler = StandardScaler()
train_features = feature_scaler.fit_transform(train_features)
test_features = feature_scaler.transform(test_features)
```

Now if you see *train_features* and *test_features,* you can see scaled values as shown below:

```
In [15]: train_features
Out[15]:
array([[ 0.83652186,  2.77984695, -1.11803399],
       [-0.31192341, -0.30949713,  0.89442719],
       [-0.05671335, -0.36014212,  0.89442719],
       [ 0.64511432, -0.15756218, -1.11803399],
       [ 1.41074449, -0.4107871 , -1.11803399],
       [-1.65177621, -0.61336704, -1.11803399],
       [ 1.0279294 , -0.51207707,  0.89442719],
       [-1.26896113, -0.46143209,  0.89442719],
       [-0.63093598,  0.04501776,  0.89442719]])

In [16]: test_features
Out[16]:
array([[ 0.45370677, -0.10691719,  0.89442719],
       [ 0.19849671,  0.2475977 ,  0.89442719],
       [-1.33276364,  0.01278914, -1.11803399]])
```

There is no need to scale labels for classification problems. For regression problems we will see how to scale labels in regression section.

## *Conclusion*

In this chapter we saw how we can preprocess data before using it for actual machine learning tasks. In the next chapter we will start new section i.e. Regression. The first machine learning algorithm that we will study will be linear regression.

## *Chapter 4*

## *Linear Regression*

In this chapter we will start our discussion with the first supervised machine learning algorithm i.e. Linear Regression which is a type of regression algorithm. In this chapter we will study linear regression with one variable as well as linear regression with multiple variables. Using linear regression with one variable, we will predict price of a car based on the year of manufacture. We will then move to more complex problem where we will predict the points that a basketball player can score based on height, weight, field goals and throws. However, first let's study theoretical back ground of linear regression.

## *Theory of Linear Regression*

In simple words, linear regression is an approach that identifies relationship between two or more than two variables. Mathematical, linear regression finds a linear function that maps independent variables to dependent variables. If this function is plotted on 2-D space, it results in a straight line.

Consider a scenario where we want to find relationship between the price of cars and the year of manufacture. If we plot the year on x-axis and price on y-axis, linear regression algorithm will find a straight line that best fits the data points. This is shown in the figure below:

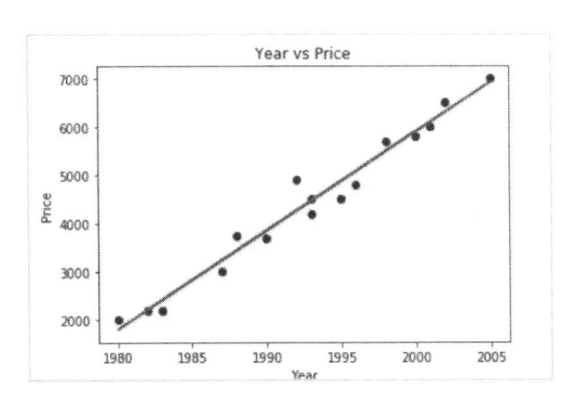

We know that straight line can be represented as:

$$b = ax_1 + c$$

Here b is the dependent variable, *a* is the slope of the line, *x* is the independent variable and c is the y intercept.

If we look at the equation we can see that b and x remain constant since they are the data variables. Therefore, linear regression algorithm gives us the slope and the intercept that best result in line which best fits the dataset.

This concept can be extended to more than one independent variable. The equation for linear regression function will then be represented as:

$$b = a_1x_1 + a_2x_2 + a_3x_3 + \ldots\ldots a_nx_n + c$$

Here is n is the total number of independent variables. This equation basically represents a hyper plane with n-dimension. It is important to mention that in two-dimensions linear regression model can be represented as a straight line. In three dimensions, it is represented in the form of plane and in more than three dimensions; it is represented as hyper plane.

Enough of the theory, let's implement linear regression with the help of Python's Scikit learn library.

## *Linear Regression with One Variable*

For the sake of simplicity, we will first implement linear regression with one variable. It is also known as Univariate Linear Regression. In this case, there is only one independent and one dependent variable.

In this section we will use the *"car_price.csv"* to predict the price of car (dependent variable) based on the year of manufacture (independent variable). You can find the dataset in the supplementary "Datasets" folder.

To predict the price, we will use linear regression algorithm implemented via Python Scikit Learn Library. So, let the fun begin:

### 1- Importing Required Libraries

As discussed in the previous chapter, the first step in implementing any machine learning algorithm is to import required libraries into your program. The following code imports required libraries:

```
import pandas as pd
import numpy as np
import matplotlib.pyplot as plt
%matplotlib inline
```

This script is implemented using Jupyter notebook. Therefore, to draw graphs within the notebook, we have used the command %matplotlib inline. If you are using Spyder, you can remove the last line.

### 2- Importing the Dataset

Once you imported the libraries, the next step is to import the dataset that you are going to use for training the algorithm. We will be using "car_price.csv" dataset. Execute the following script to import the dataset:

```
car_data = pd.read_csv('D:\Datasets\car_price.csv')
```

The script above reads the dataset and stores it in *car_data dataframe*.

### 3- Analyzing the Data

Before using the data for training, it is always a good practice to analyze your data for any missing values or scaling.

Let's first take a general look of our data. The *head* function returns the first 5 rows of the dataset. Execute the following script:

```
car_data.head()
```

|   | Year | Price |
|---|------|-------|
| 0 | 1980 | 2000  |
| 1 | 1985 | 3000  |
| 2 | 1983 | 2200  |
| 3 | 1990 | 3700  |
| 4 | 1995 | 4500  |

Similarly, the describe function returns all the statistical details of the dataset.

```
car_data.describe()
```

|       | Year        | Price       |
|-------|-------------|-------------|
| count | 20.000000   | 20.000000   |
| mean  | 1992.100000 | 4302.500000 |
| std   | 7.319045    | 1458.592959 |
| min   | 1980.000000 | 2000.000000 |
| 25%   | 1986.500000 | 3075.000000 |
| 50%   | 1992.500000 | 4350.000000 |
| 75%   | 1998.250000 | 5325.000000 |
| max   | 2005.000000 | 7000.000000 |

Finally let us see if linear regression algorithm is actually suitable for this task. Let's plot our data points on the graph and see if we can see some sort of linear relation between price and year. Execute the following script:

```
plt.scatter(car_data['Year'], car_data['Price'])
plt.title("Year vs Price")
plt.xlabel("Year")
plt.ylabel("Price")
plt.show()
```

The output of the script above looks like this:

Year vs Price

In the script above, we use the scatter plot from the *matplotlib* library to plot year on x and price on y axis. From the output figure we can clearly see that with the increase in year number the price of car increase.
There is a linear relationship between the year and price. Therefore, we can use linear regression algorithm to solve this problem.

### 4- Data Preprocessing

In the last chapter, we studied that before we feed the data to learning algorithms, we first have to divide the data into feature and label set and then test and training set. In this step we will perform these two tasks.

To divide the data into features and labels, execute the following script:

```
features=
car_data.iloc[:,0:1].values
labels=
car_data.iloc[:,1].values
```

Since we have only two columns, the 0th column contains the feature set while the 1st column contains the labels.

Finally let's divide the data into 80 % training and 20% test sets:

```
from sklearn.model_selection import train_test_split
train_features,
test_features, train_labels,
test_labels =
train_test_split(features,
labels, test_size = 0.2,
random_state = 0)
```

If we look at the dataset we can see that there is not a very huge difference between values of years and prices. Both of them have in thousands. Therefore, there is no need to scale the data and we can use this data as it is for training the algorithm.

## 5- Training the Algorithm and making Predictions

The *LinearRegression* class of the *sklearn.linear_model* is used to implement linear regression in Python. The LinearRegression class has fit method that takes training features and labels as input and train the model as shown below:

```
from sklearn.linear_model import LinearRegression
lin_reg = LinearRegression()
lin_reg.fit(train_features, train_labels)
```

Let's see what the coefficient is found by our model for the only independent variable. Execute the following script:

```
print(lin_reg.coef_)
```

The result will be: 204.815

This shows that for a unit change in year, the value of Car price increases by 204.815

Once the model is trained the final step is to predict the out of the new instance. The *predict* method of the *LinearRegression* class can be used for this purpose. The method takes test features as input and predicts the corresponding labels as output.

Execute the following script to predict the label for the test features:

```
predictions =
lin_reg.predict(
test_features)
```

All the predictions are stored in the *predictions* variable.

Let's compare the predicted value with the actual values. Execute the following script to do so:

```
comparison=pd.DataFrame({'Rea
l':test_labels,
'Predictions':predictions})

print(comparison)
```

The output looks like this:

|   | Predictions | Real |
|---|---|---|
| 0 | 5689.172831 | 5200 |
| 1 | 2821.751476 | 3000 |
| 2 | 2616.935665 | 3100 |
| 3 | 3641.014720 | 4000 |

We can see that there are four values in the test set which is 20% of the whole dataset as specified in the *train_test_split*. You can see our values are close but not exact.

To evaluate performance of a machine learning model, three metrics are commonly used: Mean Absolute Error (MAE), Mean Squared Error (MSE) and Root Mean Squared Error (RMSE). Luckily we don't have to code the complex mathematics behind these metrics. The metrics class of the *sklearn* library contains functions that can be used to find values for these metrics. Execute the following script to find MAE, MSE and RMSE for our linear regression model.

```
from sklearn import metrics
```

```python
print('MAE:',
metrics.mean_absolute_error(test_labels, predictions))
print('MSE:',
metrics.mean_squared_error(test_labels, predictions))
print('RMSE:',
np.sqrt(metrics.mean_squared_error(test_labels, predictions)))
```

The output is always follows:

```
MAE: 377.367742659
MSE: 158321.044602
RMSE: 397.895771028
```

Normally if the value of MAE and RMSE is less than 10% of the mean value for the predicted column, the algorithm performance is considered a good. However lesser the values of MAE and RMSE, higher will be the performance of the algorithm. In our case the values of MAE and RMSE are 377.36 and 397.85 which is lesser than 10% of the mean value of Price which is 430.2.

Hence we can say that our algorithm performance is good.

## *Linear Regression with Multiple Variables*

Linear regression with multiple variable or multivariate linear regression involves more than one independent variables. In this section we will use Python's *Scikit* Learn library to implement Multivariate linear regression.

We will predict how much points can a player score in a basketball match based on his height, weight, percentage of successful field goals out of all attempts, percentage of successful throws out of all attempts. We have downloaded the dataset and it is available in the Datasets folder. The dataset can also be downloaded from this link:

http://college.cengage.com/mathematics/brase/understandable_statistics/7e/students/datasets/mlr/frames/frame.html

We will follow almost same steps for this problem that we followed for single variable linear regression. We will start with importing libraries and dataset, followed by data analysis and preprocessing. Finally we will train our linear regression algorithm and will evaluate its performance.

### 1- Importing Required Libraries

The following code imports required libraries:

```
import pandas as pd
import numpy as np
import matplotlib.pyplot as plt
%matplotlib inline
```

### 2- Importing the Dataset

Though the dataset is available online, we have downloaded it an added it in the dataset repository available with this book. The dataset name is "player.csv'. Execute the following command to import the dataset.

```
player_data =
pd.read_csv('D:\Datasets\play
er.csv')
```

The script above reads the dataset and stores it in *player_data dataframe*.

### 3- Analyzing the Data

Execute the following script to eyeball the data:

```
player_data.head()
```

The output looks like this:

|   | Height | Weight | Field_Goals | Throws | Points |
|---|--------|--------|-------------|--------|--------|
| 0 | 6.8    | 225    | 0.442       | 0.672  | 9.2    |
| 1 | 6.3    | 180    | 0.435       | 0.797  | 11.7   |
| 2 | 6.4    | 190    | 0.456       | 0.761  | 15.8   |
| 3 | 6.2    | 180    | 0.416       | 0.651  | 8.6    |
| 4 | 6.9    | 205    | 0.449       | 0.900  | 23.2   |

Execute the following script to get the statistical details of the

```
player_data.describe()
```

|  | Height | Weight | Field_Goals | Throws | Points |
|---|---|---|---|---|---|
| count | 54.000000 | 54.000000 | 54.000000 | 54.000000 | 54.000000 |
| mean | 6.587037 | 209.907407 | 0.449111 | 0.741852 | 11.790741 |
| std | 0.458894 | 30.265036 | 0.056551 | 0.100146 | 5.899257 |
| min | 5.700000 | 105.000000 | 0.291000 | 0.244000 | 2.800000 |
| 25% | 6.225000 | 185.000000 | 0.415250 | 0.713000 | 8.150000 |
| 50% | 6.650000 | 212.500000 | 0.443500 | 0.753500 | 10.750000 |
| 75% | 6.900000 | 235.000000 | 0.483500 | 0.795250 | 13.600000 |
| max | 7.600000 | 263.000000 | 0.599000 | 0.900000 | 27.400000 |

### 4- Data Preprocessing

To following script divides the data into feature and label set.

```
features = 
player_data[['Height','Weight','Field_Goals','Throws']]
labels = 
player_data['Points']
```

It is important to mention that in addition to using iloc function of the dataframe, you can also divide the data into feature and label set by specifying the name of the columns as shown in the above script.

Finally let's divide the data into 80 % training and 20% test sets:

```
from sklearn.model_selection
import train_test_split

train_features,
test_features, train_labels,
test_labels =
train_test_split(features,
labels, test_size = 0.2,
random_state = 0)
```

### 5- Scaling the Data

If look at the dataset it is not scaled well, for instance the *Field_Goals* and *Throws* column have values between 0 and 1, while the rest of the columns have higher values. Therefore, before training the algorithm, we will scale our data down. Remember we discussed scaling in the last chapter. Here we will use the standard scalar class.

```
from sklearn.preprocessing
import StandardScaler

feature_scaler =
StandardScaler()

train_features =
feature_scaler.fit_transform(
train_features)
```

```
test_features =
feature_scaler.transform(test
_features)
```

## 6- Training the Algorithm and making Predictions

For multivariate linear regression, we will again use the same *LinearRegression* class of the *sklearn.linear_model* library. Execute the following script to train the model

```
from sklearn.linear_model import LinearRegression
lin_reg = LinearRegression()
lin_reg.fit(train_features,
train_labels)
```

Let's see what the coefficient is found by our model for the only independent variable. Execute the following script:

```
coefficients=
pd.DataFrame(lin_reg.coef_,fe
atures.columns,columns=['Coef
ficients'])
```

```
print(coefficients)
```

The output looks like this:

|  | Coefficients |
| --- | --- |
| Height | -2.582632 |
| Weight | 1.294067 |
| Field_Goals | 2.879289 |
| Throws | 1.035310 |

The output shows that for unit increase in Height, there is a decrease of 2.58 percent in the point scored by the player. Similarly for unit increase in weight, the number of points scored increase by 1.29 and so on.

This shows that for a unit change in year, the value of Car price increases by 204.815

Once the model is trained the final step is to predict the out of the new instance. The *predict* method of the *LinearRegression* class can be used for this purpose.

Execute the following script to predict the label for the test features:

```
predictions =
lin_reg.predict(
test_features)
```

To compare predictions with real outputs, execute the following script:

Let's compare the predicted value with the actual values. Execute the following script to do so:

```
comparison=pd.DataFrame({'Rea
l':test_labels,
'Predictions':predictions})
print(comparison)
```

The output looks like this:

|    | Predictions | Real |
|----|-------------|------|
| 53 | 10.342831   | 8.3  |
| 33 | 11.431936   | 7.2  |
| 48 | 9.637807    | 2.8  |
| 26 | 14.690648   | 5.6  |
| 11 | 14.363039   | 9.1  |
| 2  | 12.763432   | 15.8 |
| 32 | 14.397398   | 9.6  |
| 42 | 14.473602   | 15.4 |
| 45 | 7.550197    | 7.9  |
| 30 | 14.867451   | 11.7 |
| 4  | 11.721830   | 23.2 |

From the output, you can see that the predicted values are not really close to the actual values.

Execute the following script to find MAE, MSE and RMSE for our linear regression model.

```
from sklearn import metrics
print('MAE:', metrics.mean_absolute_error(test_labels, predictions))
print('MSE:', metrics.mean_squared_error(test_labels, predictions))
print('RMSE:', np.sqrt(metrics.mean_squared_error(test_labels, predictions)))
```

The output is always follows:

```
MAE: 4.65654985924
MSE: 32.1977246142
RMSE: 5.67430388808
```

RMSE are 4.65 and 5.67 which is greater than 10% of the mean value of point which is 1.179 Hence, we can say that our algorithm is not performing good on this dataset. There are many reasons why an algorithm can perform poorly and how to improve the performance and algorithm which we will discuss in a later chapter.

## Conclusion

In this chapter, we studied our first supervised algorithm i.e. linear regression. We saw what univariate and multivariate linear regressions are and how they can be implemented via Python Scikit learn library. In the next chapter, we will study Polynomial Regression which is basically non-linear regression.

*Chapter 5*

*Polynomial Regression*

In the last chapter we studied how linear regression algorithm can be used to find the straight line that best fits the data points. However, in real world, data is not always linearly related. For instance if you take a look at the data distribution in the following figure

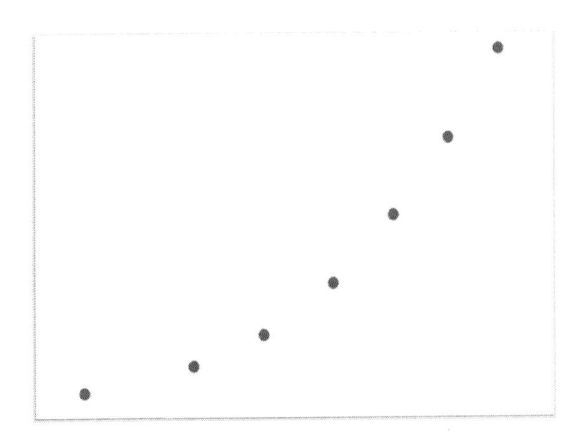

Here if we draw a straight line that best fits the data points, some points will end up above the line the other would end up below the line as shown in the following figure. In such a case, the chance of error in prediction will be higher.

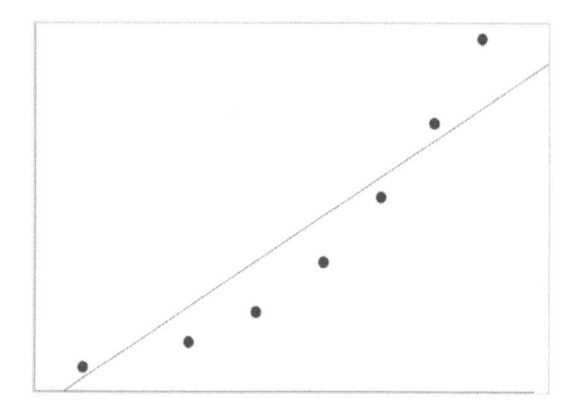

On the other hand if we have a curved line that fits all the data points as shown in the following figure, the chance of error can be minimized.

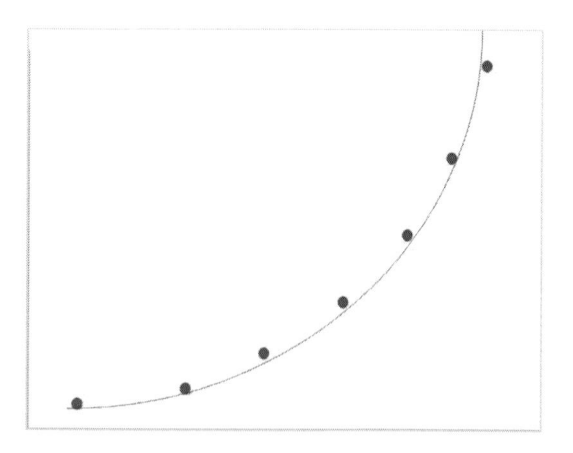

In polynomial regression we try to find models that are not straight lines but they fit the data points more accurately.

In the last chapter we discussed that the straight linear model can be represented as:

$$B = a_1x_1 + a_2x_2 + a_3x_3 + \ldots\ldots\ldots\ldots A_nx_n$$

On the other hand, polynomial regression results in a mode of degree greater than 1 e.g

$$B = a_1x_1^2 + a_2x_2^3 + a_3x_3^2 + \ldots\ldots\ldots\ldots A_nx_n^5$$

## *Polynomial Regression with Python Scikit Learn*

Let's implement polynomial regression with Python Scikit Learn. The problem that we are going to solve in this section is to predict the consumption of gas( in millions) in the 48 states of US based on features such as paved highways (miles), petrol tax (cents), per capita income, and ratio of individuals with driving license.

For further details of the dataset, visit this link. The data can be downloaded from the link as well, however the data is not in CSV format at the download link. For the ease of the readers, the data has been downloaded, converted to CSV and saved in the Datasets folder with name "petrol_data.csv" you can found it there.

As always, the first step is to import the required libraries:

### 1- Importing Required Libraries

The following code imports required libraries:

```
import pandas as pd
```

```
import numpy as np
import matplotlib.pyplot as plt
%matplotlib inline
```

This script is implemented using Jupyter notebook. Therefore, to draw graphs within the notebook, we have used the command %matplotlib inline. If you are using Spyder, you can remove the last line.

### 2- Importing the Dataset

Execute the following command to import the dataset.

```
petrol_data = pd.read_csv('D:\Datasets\petrol_data.csv')
```

The script above reads the dataset and stores it in *player_data dataframe*.

### 3- Analyzing the Data

Execute the following script to eyeball the data:

```
petrol_data.head()
```

The output looks like this:

|   | Petrol_tax | Average_income | Paved_Highways | Population_Driver_licence(%) | Petrol_Consumption |
|---|---|---|---|---|---|
| 0 | 9.0 | 3571 | 1976 | 0.525 | 541 |
| 1 | 9.0 | 4092 | 1250 | 0.572 | 524 |
| 2 | 9.0 | 3865 | 1586 | 0.580 | 561 |
| 3 | 7.5 | 4870 | 2351 | 0.529 | 414 |
| 4 | 8.0 | 4399 | 431 | 0.544 | 410 |

Execute the following script to get the statistical details of the

```
petrol_data.describe()
```

|   | Petrol_tax | Average_income | Paved_Highways | Population_Driver_licence(%) | Petrol_Consumption |
|---|---|---|---|---|---|
| count | 48.000000 | 48.000000 | 48.000000 | 48.000000 | 48.000000 |
| mean | 7.668333 | 4241.833333 | 5565.416667 | 0.570333 | 576.770833 |
| std | 0.950770 | 573.623768 | 3491.507166 | 0.055470 | 111.885816 |
| min | 5.000000 | 3063.000000 | 431.000000 | 0.451000 | 344.000000 |
| 25% | 7.000000 | 3739.000000 | 3110.250000 | 0.529750 | 509.500000 |
| 50% | 7.500000 | 4298.000000 | 4735.500000 | 0.564500 | 568.500000 |
| 75% | 8.125000 | 4578.750000 | 7156.000000 | 0.595250 | 632.750000 |
| max | 10.000000 | 5342.000000 | 17782.000000 | 0.724000 | 968.000000 |

### 4- Data Preprocessing

To following script divides the data into feature and label set.

```
features = 
player_data[['Height','Weight
','Field_Goals','Throws']]
labels = 
player_data['Points']
```

Finally let's divide the data into 80 % training and 20% test sets:

```
from sklearn.model_selection
import train_test_split

train_features,
test_features, train_labels,
test_labels =
train_test_split(features,
labels, test_size = 0.2,
random_state = 0)
```

### 5- Generating Polynomial Features

To implement Polynomial Regression using Python's Scikit Learn library, the same LinearRegression class is used. However before feeding our data to the algorithm, we need to convert linear features into polynomial features i.e. feature with higher degrees. If you look at the feature set we have 4 features at the moment. If we convert these linear features to polynomial features of degree 2, we will end up with 15 features. Three features for each column, i.e. feature with degree 0, 1 and 2. We have 4 features, therefore 4 x 3 = 12. In addition we also have cross terms in polynomial regression. We have four features, therefore we will have three cross terms i.e. column1 x column2, column2 x column3 and column3xcolumn4.

Let's see how we can convert linear features to polynomial features with Python Scikit learn library. Execute the following script:

```
from sklearn.preprocessing import PolynomialFeatures
poly_reg_feat = PolynomialFeatures(degree=2)
train_features_poly = poly_reg_feat.fit_transform(train_features)
test_features_poly = poly_reg_feat.transform(test_features)
```

Take a careful look at the script above. To implement polynomial regression the *PolynomialFeature* class from the *sklearn.preprocessing* library is used. Degree of polynomial is passed to the class constructor. Next the *fit_transform* method is called and the original feature set is passed to this method. The *fit_transform* method returns polynomial feature set. Now if you check the columns of *train_feature_poly* and *test_features_poly* variables, you will see that they will contain 15 columns, instead of the original four.

### 6- Scaling the Data

It is always a good practice to scale your data in case of polynomial regression since the degree of the features is different which can result in highly un-scaled data. Therefore, before training the algorithm, we will scale our data down. Here we will use the standard scalar class.

```
from sklearn.preprocessing import StandardScaler
feature_scaler = StandardScaler()
train_features_poly = feature_scaler.fit_transform(train_features_poly)
```

```
test_features_poly =
feature_scaler.transform(test
_features_poly)
```

## 7- Training the Algorithm and making Predictions

As earlier said, for polynomial regression, we will again use the same *LinearRegression* class of the *sklearn.linear_model* library. Execute the following script to train the model

```
from sklearn.linear_model import LinearRegression

lin_reg = LinearRegression()

lin_reg.fit(train_features_po
ly, train_labels)
```

Similarly, to make predictions,

Execute the following script:

```
predictions =
lin_reg.predict(test_features
_poly)
```

Let's compare the predicted value with the actual values. Execute the following script to do so:

```
comparison=pd.DataFrame({'Real':test_labels,
'Predictions':predictions})
print(comparison)
```

The output looks like this:

|   | Predictions | Real |
|---|---|---|
| 0 | 553.577485 | 534 |
| 1 | 547.261229 | 410 |
| 2 | 577.220482 | 577 |
| 3 | 580.830717 | 571 |
| 4 | 558.903290 | 577 |
| 5 | 639.422694 | 704 |
| 6 | 568.688917 | 487 |
| 7 | 677.972568 | 587 |
| 8 | 401.726005 | 467 |
| 9 | 500.578904 | 580 |

From the output, it can be seen that if not accurate, our algorithm is still making some pretty close predictions.

### 8- Evaluating the Algorithm

As always, the last step of any machine learning process is to evaluate performance of the trained algorithm. As discussed earlier, for regression the performance is evaluated in terms of mean absolute error, mean squared error and root mean squared error. The following script finds these values for our algorithm:

```
from sklearn import metrics
print('MAE:', metrics.mean_absolute_error(test_labels, predictions))
print('MSE:', metrics.mean_squared_error(test_labels, predictions))
print('RMSE:', np.sqrt(metrics.mean_squared_error(test_labels, predictions)))
```

The output values are as follows:

```
MAE: 56.6920504483
MSE: 4933.58260557
RMSE: 70.2394661538
```

The value of MAE is 56.69 which is less than 10% of the mean value of petrol consumption 57.67. However for RMSE the value is 70.23 which means that our dataset has outliers which needs to be dealt with. Overall, the performance of our algorithm is good.

## Conclusion

In this chapter we studied Polynomial regression which is a type of supervised regression algorithm. In the next chapter, we will see how decision tree algorithm can be used for regression purposes.

## *Chapter 6*

### *Decision Tree for Regression*

In the last two chapters we studied Linear Regression and Polynomial Regression algorithms. These algorithms are based on the principle of error correction using gradient decent algorithm. In this chapter we are going to study another extremely powerful machine learning algorithm based on entropy.

The principle behind the working of a decision tree is very simple. Each feature in the dataset is treated as a node in the decision tree. At each node a decision is made regarding which path to choose in the tree depending upon the value of the feature at that particular node. The process continues until the leaf node is reached. Leaf node contains the final decision.

This explanation might seem daunting at first but we have been using decision trees all our life. Suppose there is a bank that has to decide whether loan should be given to a particular customer or not. The bank has customer data including age, gender and salary. Bank has to decide whether the customer should be give loan or not.

A bank may define criteria which consists of set of rules that defines whether the loan will be awarded or not. These rules can look like this.

1. If the age of the customer is greater than 25 and less than 60, then go to next step. Else simply reject the loan application.
2. If the first condition is satisfied, then check if the person is salaried or not.

If the person is salaried, go to step 3 else if the person is jobless, reject the loan application.
3. If the person is salaried and gender is male, go to step 4. Else if the gender is female go to step 5.
4. If the salary is greater than 35000 dollars per year, award the loan else reject the application.
5. If the salary is greater than 45000 dollars per year, award the loan else reject the application.

The decision tree based on such rules looks like this:

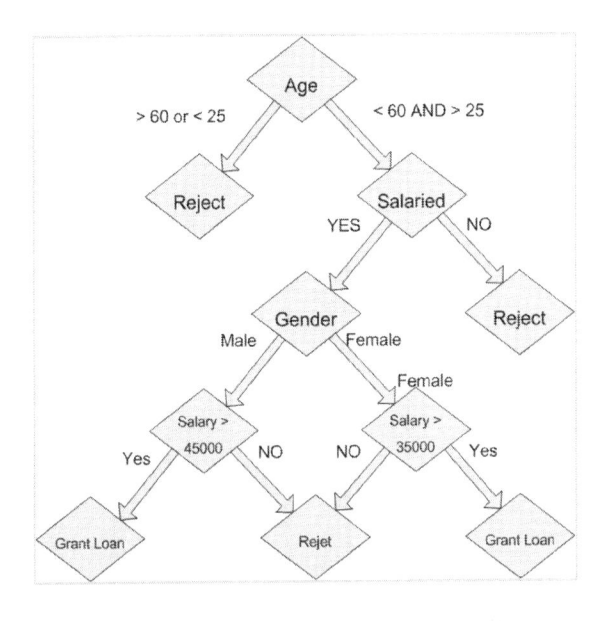

The above set of rules is very simplistic and is chosen randomly. In real world the data is much more complex and statistical techniques such as entropy are used to create these nodes. Entropy refers to the impurity of classification in the labeled data. Basically in decision trees, the feature that results in minimum entropy in the output labels is set at root node. For instance, if 95% of the times when the age is greater than 60 and less than 25, the application for loan is rejected, the impurity in the output will be 5% for Age with values between 60 and 25. Similarly, if in 80 of the cases the loan for jobless person is rejected, the impurity in the output label for salaried attribute will be 20%. As a rule of thumb, the features with lesser impurity are placed higher in the tree nodes.

## *Benefits of Decision Trees*

Decision trees can be very handy because of their simplicity and ease of understanding. Following are some of the advantages of decision tree algorithm.

1- Decision trees work equally well for regression as well as classification tasks which means that you can predict continuous as well as discrete values.
2- Decision trees can be used to classify linear as well as non-linear data.

3- In comparison to most of the other machine learning algorithms, they are relatively faster to train.

## *Using Python Scikit Learn Library to Implement Decision Trees*

As always, we will use Python's Scikit Learn Library to see decision trees in action. In this section we will again predict the consumption of petrol ( in millions) in the 48 states of US based on features such as paved highways (miles), petrol tax (cents), per capita income, and ratio of individuals with driving license.

For further details of the dataset, visit this link. The data can be downloaded from the link as well; however the data is not in CSV format at the download link. For the ease of the readers, the data has been downloaded, converted to CSV and saved in the Datasets folder with name "petrol_data.csv" you can found it there.

Now you should be familiar with the machine learning process. The first step to solve every machine learning problem with Python is to import the required libraries. The following script does that:

### 1. Importing Necessary Libraries

```
import pandas as pd
import numpy as np
import matplotlib.pyplot as plt
%matplotlib inline
```

This script is implemented using Jupyter notebook. Therefore, to draw graphs within the notebook, we have used the command %matplotlib inline. If you are using Spyder, you can remove the last line.

### 2. Importing Dataset

Execute the following command to import the dataset.

```
petrol_data = pd.read_csv('D:\Datasets\petrol_data.csv')
```

The script above reads the dataset and stores it in *player_data dataframe*.

## 3. Data Analysis

Execute the following script to eyeball the data:

```
petrol_data.head()
```

The result looks like this:

| | Petrol_tax | Average_income | Paved_Highways | Population_Driver_licence(%) | Petrol_Consumption |
|---|---|---|---|---|---|
| 0 | 9.0 | 3571 | 1976 | 0.525 | 541 |
| 1 | 9.0 | 4092 | 1250 | 0.572 | 524 |
| 2 | 9.0 | 3865 | 1586 | 0.580 | 561 |
| 3 | 7.5 | 4870 | 2351 | 0.529 | 414 |
| 4 | 8.0 | 4399 | 431 | 0.544 | 410 |

## 4. Data Preprocessing

To following script divides the data into feature and label set.

```
features= petrol_data.iloc[:,0:4].values
labels= petrol_data.iloc[:,4].values
```

Finally let's divide the data into 80 % training and 20% test sets:

```
from sklearn.model_selection import train_test_split
train_features, test_features, train_labels, test_labels = train_test_split(features, labels, test_size = 0.2, random_state = 0)
```

### 5. Data Scaling

If you look at the dataset, you can see that our data is not very well scaled. For instance, the feature *Population_Driver_License* has values between 0 and 1 while Average_Income and Paved_Highways has values in thousand. Therefore, before feeding our data to the algorithm, we need to scale our features. Execute the following script to do so:

```
from sklearn.preprocessing import StandardScaler
```

```
feature_scaler =
StandardScaler()
train_features_poly =
feature_scaler.fit_transform(
train_features)
test_features_poly =
feature_scaler.transform(test
_features)
```

### 6. Training the Algorithm

We have scaled our features down. Now is the time to train our algorithm. To implement decision tree for classification, we use the *DecisionTreeClassifier* class of the *sklearn.tree* library. The fit method of the class is used to train the algorithm. The training features and labels are passed to this fit as shown in the following script:

```
from sklearn.tree import
DecisionTreeClassifier
dt_reg =
DecisionTreeClassifier()
dt_reg.fit(train_features,
train_labels)
```

### 7. Make Predictions

Finally to make predictions we will use the predict method of the DecisionTreeClassifier class object dt_reg that we created in the last section. Test features will be passed to it as a parameter.

```
predictions = dt_reg.predict(test_features)
```

Let's compare the predicted values with the actual values, execute the following script:

```
comparison=pd.DataFrame({'Real':test_labels,
'Predictions':predictions})
print(comparison)
```

The output of the script above looks like this:

|   | Predictions | Real |
|---|---|---|
| 0 | 591 | 534 |
| 1 | 714 | 410 |
| 2 | 566 | 577 |
| 3 | 547 | 571 |
| 4 | 566 | 577 |
| 5 | 566 | 704 |
| 6 | 591 | 487 |
| 7 | 610 | 587 |
| 8 | 460 | 467 |
| 9 | 464 | 580 |

## 8. Evaluating the Algorithm

The following script finds these values of mean absolute error, mean squared error and root mean squared error

```
from sklearn import metrics
print('MAE:',
metrics.mean_absolute_error(t
est_labels, predictions))
print('MSE:',
metrics.mean_squared_error(te
st_labels, predictions))
print('RMSE:',
np.sqrt(metrics.mean_squared_
error(test_labels,
predictions)))
```

The output values are as follows:

```
MAE: 79.5
MSE: 14037.7
RMSE: 118.480800132
```

The value of MAE is 79, which is greater than MAE value calculated for Polynomial Regression algorithm in the last chapter. Similarly, the value of RMSE in the case of decision tree is 118 which is far greater than the value obtained using polynomial regression algorithm in the last chapter. Hence we can say that for predicting petrol prices given the dataset used in this chapter, Polynomial regression algorithm outperforms the Decision tree algorithm.

**Conclusion**

In this chapter we studied what decision tree algorithm is and how it can be used for regression. In the next chapter we will study Random Forest algorithm which is basically based on decision tree algorithm.

# Chapter 7

## *Random Forest for Regression*

In the last chapter we studied decision trees. A single decision tree can be biased depending upon the data. A better approach could be to use multiple decision trees that make their own prediction and then final prediction can be calculating by finding the average of all predictions made by all the trees. This approach is known as ensemble learning. In ensemble learning multiple algorithms of same or different types are joined together to create a more power machine learning model. Random forest is a type of ensemble learning models and can be used for supervised machine learning.

Random forest algorithm unites multiple decision tree algorithms, creating a forest. Therefore, the algorithm is called "Random Forest" algorithm. Like decision tree algorithm, random forest algorithm can be used to predict continuous values (regression) as well as discrete values (classification). In this article we will implement random forest algorithm with the help of Python's Scikit learn library for regression purpose. We will see how we can use random forest algorithm for Classification in the Classification section of the book.

## *Working of Random Forest Algorithm*

Random forest algorithm performs following steps:

1. Choose K random data points from the dataset
2. Create a decision tree regression or classification algorithm based on the K data points.

3. Select the number of trees for random forest algorithm and perform steps 1 and 2 on each tree.
4. If the problem is regression, each tree predicts a continuous value; the final output can be calculated by taking mean of the values predicted by all the trees. If the problem at hand is classification problem, each tree predicts a discrete value. Final category can be selected by majority voting.

## *Pros of Random Forest Algorithm*

There are several advantages of random forest algorithm, some of which have been enlisted below:

1. A random forest algorithm is one of the most stable algorithm and scales very well. Since there are multiple trees in the forest, introduction or removal of data from the dataset can impact a small portion of trees

but not all trees. The overall stability of the algorithm is not affected.
2. Random forest algorithm performs equally well in case of numerical as well as categorical features.
3. You don't need to perform feature scaling in case of random forest algorithm since it doesn't rely on the distance between the data points in the feature space.

## *Cons of Random Forest Algorithm*

1. One of the biggest disadvantages of random forest algorithm is its complexity. Since hundreds or sometimes thousands of trees are involved in prediction, it is not easy to understand how the final prediction was made.

2. The complexity of an algorithm comes with the cost of time. Random forest algorithm can take a lot of time to execute depending

upon the number of trees in the forest.

## *Implementing Random Forest Algorithm using Scikit Learn*

In this section, we will use random forest algorithm to predict how much points can a player score in a basketball match based on his height, weight, percentage of successful field goals out of all attempts, percentage of successful throws out of all attempts. We have downloaded the dataset and it is available in the Datasets folder.

We will follow the same steps that we have been following in all the last chapters.

### 1- Importing Required Libraries

The following code imports required libraries:

```
import pandas as pd
import numpy as np
```

```
import matplotlib.pyplot as plt
%matplotlib inline
```

### 2- Importing the Dataset

Though the dataset is available online, we have downloaded it and added it in the dataset repository available with this book. The dataset name is "player.csv'. Execute the following command to import the dataset.

```
player_data = pd.read_csv('D:\Datasets\player.csv')
```

The script above reads the dataset and stores it in *player_data dataframe*.

### 3- Analyzing the Data

Execute the following script to eyeball the data:

```
player_data.head()
```

The output looks like this:

|   | Height | Weight | Field_Goals | Throws | Points |
|---|---|---|---|---|---|
| 0 | 6.8 | 225 | 0.442 | 0.672 | 9.2 |
| 1 | 6.3 | 180 | 0.435 | 0.797 | 11.7 |
| 2 | 6.4 | 190 | 0.456 | 0.761 | 15.8 |
| 3 | 6.2 | 180 | 0.416 | 0.651 | 8.6 |
| 4 | 6.9 | 205 | 0.449 | 0.900 | 23.2 |

### 4- Data Preprocessing

To following script divides the data into feature and label set.

```
features = player_data.iloc[:, 0:4].values
labels = player_data.iloc[:, 4].values
```

Finally let's divide the data into 80 % training and 20% test sets:

```
from sklearn.model_selection import train_test_split
train_features, test_features, train_labels, test_labels = train_test_split(features,
```

```
labels, test_size = 0.2,
random_state = 0)
```

### 5- Scaling the Data

If you look at the dataset it is not scaled well, for instance the Field_Goals and Throws column have values between 0 and 1, while the rest of the columns have higher values. Therefore, before training the algorithm, we will scale our data down. Remember we discussed scaling Chapter 3. Here we will use the standard scalar class.

```
from sklearn.preprocessing import StandardScaler
feature_scaler = StandardScaler()
train_features = feature_scaler.fit_transform(train_features)
test_features = feature_scaler.transform(test_features)
```

### 6- Training the Algorithm and making Predictions

To implement Random Forest Algorithm for regression tasks, the *RandomForestRegressor* class is of the *sklear.ensemble* library is used. The number of trees is passed as argument to the n_estimator parameter. In the following script the number of script is set to 200.

```
from sklearn.ensemble import RandomForestRegressor

rf_reg = RandomForestRegressor(n_estimators=200, random_state=0)
rf_reg.fit(train_features, train_labels)
```

Execute the following script to predict the label for the test features:

```
predictions = rf_reg.predict(test_features)
```

To compare predictions with real outputs, execute the following script:

Let's compare the predicted value with the actual values. Execute the following script to do so:

```
comparison=pd.DataFrame({'Real':test_labels,
'Predictions':predictions})
print(comparison)
```

The output looks like this:

|    | Predictions | Real |
|----|-------------|------|
| 0  | 10.6050     | 8.3  |
| 1  | 9.5780      | 7.2  |
| 2  | 10.0470     | 2.8  |
| 3  | 19.6975     | 5.6  |
| 4  | 16.0445     | 9.1  |
| 5  | 13.2735     | 15.8 |
| 6  | 12.8185     | 9.6  |
| 7  | 14.1255     | 15.4 |
| 8  | 11.8640     | 7.9  |
| 9  | 13.5840     | 11.7 |
| 10 | 13.9590     | 23.2 |

### 7- Evaluating the Algorithm

Execute the following script to find MAE, MSE and RMSE for our linear regression model.

```
from sklearn import metrics
print('MAE:',
metrics.mean_absolute_error(t
est_labels, predictions))
print('MSE:',
metrics.mean_squared_error(te
st_labels, predictions))
print('RMSE:',
np.sqrt(metrics.mean_squared_
error(test_labels,
predictions)))
```

The output is always follows:

```
MAE: 5.00731818182
MSE: 39.4070574773
RMSE: 6.27750408023
```

The value of MAE is 5.00, which is greater than MAE value calculated for Linear Regression algorithm in Chapter 4 i.e. 4.65. Similarly, the value of RMSE in the case of Random Forest algorithm is 6.27, which is greater than 5.67, i.e. the value obtained using Linear Regression algorithm in Chapter 4. Hence we can say that for predicting point scored by a basketball player given the dataset used in this chapter, Linear Regression algorithm outperforms the Random Forest algorithm.

# Chapter 8

## *Support Vector Regression*

Support Vector Regression (SVR) is a type of Support Vector Machines (SVM) Algorithm and can be used for performing linear as well as non-linear regression. Introduced in 1960's SVM is one of the most famous supervised machine learning algorithms. Before neural networks became common, SVM was said to be the most accurate machine learning algorithm.

In this chapter we will briefly review the intuition behind SVM algorithm and how they actually work. Since we are in regression section, we will implement SVR algorithm using Python library to predict the price of a car based on the year. But first let's study the theory behind SVM.

## *SVM Theory*

For typical linear regression in two dimensional feature space, the task is to find a straight line that successfully bisects the data points. However in real world, there can be multiple decision boundaries that can successfully classify the data points as shown in Fig1.

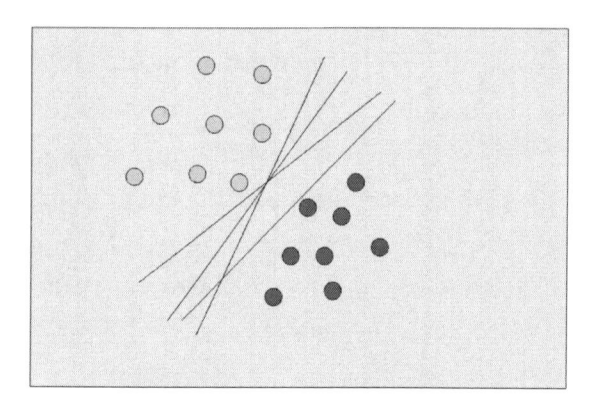

Fig1: Multiple boundaries

However whether a new data point will be successfully classified or not depends upon the decision boundary chosen for classification.

For instance take a look at Fig2. Suppose we have to classify new data point i.e. the Red Circle. If we have the decision boundary as in Fig2, the new data point will be classified as blue.

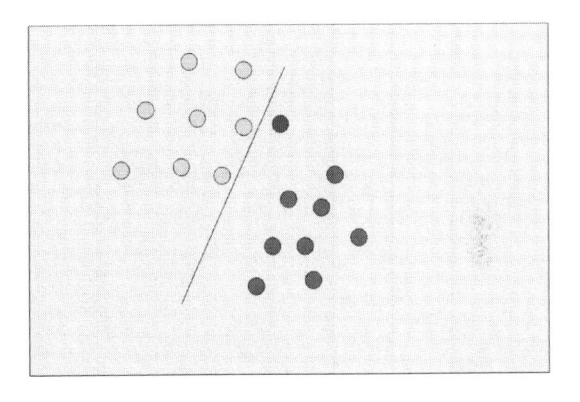

Fig2: New data point classified as blue

On the other hand if we have the decision boundary as in Fig3, the new data point will be classified as yellow as shown below:

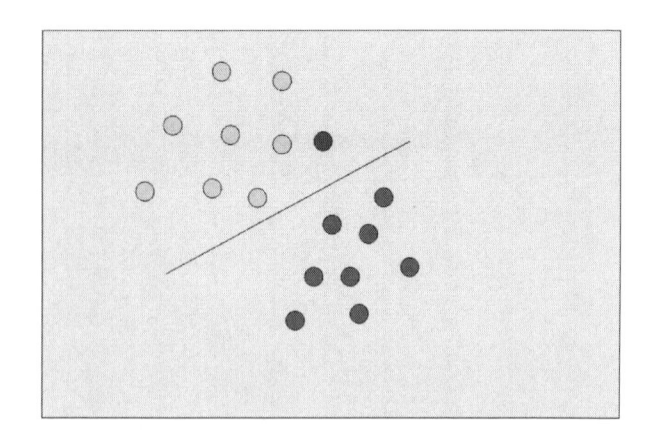

Fig3: New data point classified as yellow

From Fig2 and Fig3, it can be clearly seen that there can be multiple decision boundaries that successfully classify a dataset. However, not all of them are optimal. Given a new data point, different decision boundaries may classify data differently.

The job of SVM algorithm is to find the decision boundary that classifies data in such a way that the chances of misclassification can be minimized. SVM algorithm does so by maximizing the distance between the closest data points from all the classes in the dataset.

The SVM algorithm finds such a boundary with the help of support vectors, hence the name Support Vector Machines. Support vectors are the vectors that pass through the closest data points of the two classes to classify. The job is to maximize the distance between these two vectors. A line parallel to both these support vectors is drawn in the middle of these support vectors. This decision boundary is considered the most optimal decision boundary. The decision boundary found by Support Vector along with support vector machines looks like the one in Fig4.

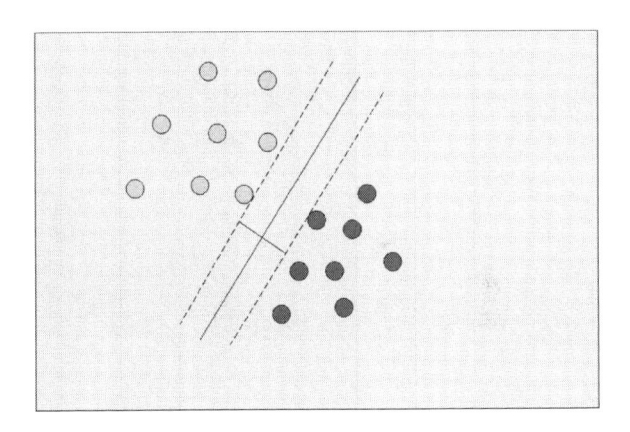

Fig4: Decision boundary with Support Vectors

Enough of the theory, now let's see how we can use Support Vector regression which is a type of SVM to predict price of a car based on year it was manufactured. We will use Python's Scikit Learn Library for that.

## *Implementing SVR with Python Scikit Learn*

In this section we will use the *"car_price.csv"* dataset to predict the price of car (dependent variable) based on the year of manufacture (independent variable). You can find the dataset in the supplementary "Datasets" folder.

### 1- Importing Required Libraries

The following code imports required libraries:

```
import pandas as pd
import numpy as np
```

```
import matplotlib.pyplot as plt
%matplotlib inline
```

This script is implemented using Jupyter notebook. Therefore, to draw graphs within the notebook, we have used the command %matplotlib inline. If you are using Spyder, you can remove the last line.

### 2- Importing the Dataset

We will be using "car_price.csv" dataset. Execute the following script to import the dataset:

```
car_data = pd.read_csv('D:\Datasets\car_price.csv')
```

The script above reads the dataset and stores it in *car_data dataframe*.

### 3- Analyzing the Data

Let's first take a general look of our data. The *head* function returns the first 5 rows of the dataset. Execute the following script:

```
car_data.head()
```

|   | Year | Price |
|---|------|-------|
| 0 | 1980 | 2000  |
| 1 | 1985 | 3000  |
| 2 | 1983 | 2200  |
| 3 | 1990 | 3700  |
| 4 | 1995 | 4500  |

### 4- Data Preprocessing

To divide the data into features and labels, execute the following script:

```
features=
car_data.iloc[:,0:1].values
labels=
car_data.iloc[:,1].values
```

Finally let's divide the data into 80 % training and 20% test sets:

```
from sklearn.model_selection import train_test_split
train_features,
test_features, train_labels,
test_labels =
```

```
train_test_split(features,
labels, test_size = 0.2,
random_state = 0)
```

If you look at the dataset we can see that there is not a very huge difference between values of years and prices. Both of them have in thousands. Therefore, there is no need to scale the data and we can use this data as it is for training the algorithm.

## 5- Training the Algorithm and making Predictions

The *SVR* class of the *sklearn.svm* is used to implement support vector regression in Python. The SVR class takes a value for its kernel parameter. If your data is linear which actually is the case with car_data, then use "linear" as kernel value, else you can use any kernel value from the list given in the documentations at this link.

SVR class has fit method that takes training features and labels as input and train the model as shown below:

```
from sklearn.svm import SVR
```

```
svr_reg = 
SVR(kernel='linear')
svr_reg.fit(train_features, 
train_labels)
```

Finally, execute the following script to predict the label for the test features:

```
predictions = 
lin_reg.predict(
test_features)
```

All the predictions are stored in the *predictions* variable.

Let's compare the predicted value with the actual values. Execute the following script to do so:

```
comparison=pd.DataFrame({'Real':test_labels,
'Predictions':predictions})
print(comparison)
```

|   | Predictions | Real |
|---|---|---|
| 0 | 4945.0 | 5200 |
| 1 | 3699.0 | 3000 |
| 2 | 3610.0 | 3100 |
| 3 | 4055.0 | 4000 |

## *Evaluating the Algorithm*

Execute the following script to find MAE, MSE and RMSE for our linear regression model.

```
from sklearn import metrics
print('MAE:',
metrics.mean_absolute_error(t
est_labels, predictions))
print('MSE:',
metrics.mean_squared_error(te
st_labels, predictions))
print('RMSE:',
np.sqrt(metrics.mean_squared_
error(test_labels,
predictions)))
```

The output is always follows:

```
MAE: 379.75
MSE: 204187.75
RMSE: 451.871386569
```

The value of MAE is 379.75 in case of SVR, which is greater than MAE value calculated for Linear Regression algorithm in Chapter 4 i.e. 377.36 Similarly, the value of RMSE in the case of SVR calculate in this chapter is 451.87, which is greater than 397.89, i.e. the value obtained using Linear Regression algorithm in Chapter 4. Hence we can say that for car prices based on the year they were manufactured given the dataset used in this chapter, Linear Regression algorithm outperforms the Support Vector Regression Algorithm.

# Chapter 9

## Naïve Bayes Algorithm for Classification

In the previous chapters, we covered some of the most commonly used algorithms for regression e.g. Linear Regression, Support Vector Regression, Polynomial Regression, Decision Trees and Random Forest algorithms. Some of these algorithms have variants that can be used for classification as well which we will see in the upcoming chapters. In this chapter we will start our discussion about classification algorithms i.e. Algorithms used to predict discrete value, or a class label for input data. The first classification algorithm that we are going to cover in this section is the Naïve Bayes Algorithm.

## *Theory of Naïve Bayes (NB) Algorithm*

Naïve Bayes algorithm is a supervised machine learning algorithm based on Bayes's Theorm. NB algorithm is based on principle of feature independence which states that features within a dataset have no relation to each other. For instance a fruit may be considered as banana if it is 5 or more inches long, yellow in color and 1 cm in diameter. Naïve Bayes have no concern if these features depend on each other. The fruit is declared as a banana via independent contribution of these features. Due to this independence assumption, NB algorithm is called Naïve.

Naïve Bayes algorithm is the simplest of all the machine learning algorithms and yet very powerful.

Mathematically Bayes theorem can be represented as:

$$P(A|B) = \frac{P(B|A).P(A)}{P(B)}$$

The aforementioned terms are explained as follows:

1. P(A|B) is the probability that event A will occur given attribute set B
2. P(A) is the prior probability of the occurrence of event A
3. P(B|A) is the probability of attribute set if the event A occurs
4. P(B) is the prior probability of the occurrence of predictors

Let's understand this concept with the help of an example.

Suppose we have weight profile of 12 individuals and based on that we want to predict whether or not the patients are diabetic. The record set looks like this:

| Weight | Diabetic |
|---|---|
| Overweight | Yes |
| Normal | No |
| Underweight | No |
| Normal | Yes |
| Overweight | Yes |
| Normal | No |

| | |
|---|---|
| Underweight | No |
| Overweight | No |
| Normal | No |
| Overweight | Yes |
| Underweight | No |
| Underweight | No |

There are three steps involved in manually implementing the NB algorithm.

1- Create a frequency table for the data as shown below:

| | Yes | No |
|---|---|---|
| Overweight | 3 | 1 |
| Normal | 1 | 3 |
| Underweight | 0 | 4 |
| Total | 4 | 8 |

2- Calculate the Class/Event Prior Probability and Attribute Prior Probability

No let's calculate the prior probability of the events:

P(A) when Diabetic (Yes) = 4/12 = 0.33

P(A) when Diabetic (No) = 8/12 = 0.67

Finally let's find the prior probability of the features:

P(B) when Overweight = 4/12 = 0.33

P(B) when Normal= 4/12 = 0.33

P(B) when Underweight = 4/12 = 0.33

3- Now if a new patient comes, we have to find whether he is diabetic depending upon his weight. There can be two outcomes: diabetic or not. We will find probabilities for both. The class that results in higher probability will be assigned to the patient.

Suppose an overweight patient arrives to the clinic and we have to test him for diabetes. We need to solve two equations:

a) P(Yes|Overweight) = P(Overweight|Yes) x P(Yes) / P(Overweight)

= (0.75 X 0.33) / 0.33

= 0.75

b) P(No|Overweight) = P(Overweight|No) x P(No) / P(Overweight)

= (0.125 X 0.67) / 0.33

= 0.25

You can see that probability of being diabetic when overweight is 0.75 which is greater than probability of not being diabetic which is 0.25, therefore NB algorithm will classify this patient as diabetic.

In the above case there was only one attribute, in case of multiple attributes, the probability can be calculated as:

$$P(A|B) = P(B1|A) \times P(B2|A) \times P(B3|A) \ldots\ldots$$
$$P(BN|A) \times P(A)$$

## *Advantages of Naïve Bayes Algorithm*

1. NB algorithm is very simple and fast to train since no complex mathematics and error correction or back propagations is involved.
2. NB algorithms outperform most of the other algorithms in case of categorical data. For numeric features, NB algorithm assumes normal distribution.

## *Disadvantages of Naïve Bayes Algorithm*

1. In real world data, features are mostly dependent on other features. The independence assumption of NB algorithm makes it a bad predictor for datasets with interdependent features.

2. If a categorical feature has such a value in test set which was not seen in the training set, the NB algorithm will assign zero probability to such instance. Therefore, it is very important to cross validate results obtained using NB algorithm.
3.

## *Naïve Bayes Algorithm Applications*

1. NB algorithm is ideal for multi-class problems and is commonly employed for text classification problems such as sentimental analysis and email spam filtering.
2. NB algorithm is also widely used in combination of collaborative filtering algorithms for building machine learning based recommender systems.
3. NB is extremely fast compared to other advanced algorithms and is

therefore incorporated in real time applications.

## *Implementing Naïve Bayes Algorithm With Python Scikit Learn*

As always, in this section we will use Python's Scikit Learn library to implement the Naïve Bayes algorithm.

In Scikit Learn you can implement three variants of NB algorithm:

1- Guassian NB: Use feature has normal data distribution
2- Multinomial NB: Use when your features contain discrete data
3- Bernoulli: Use when your features contain binary data.

In this section, we will predict the type of the iris flower based on four attributes: sepal length, sepal width, petal length and petal width.

More details of the IRIS dataset can be found at this link:

https://archive.ics.uci.edu/ml/datasets/Iris

The dataset has been supplied with the book and can be found by the name of iris_data.csv in the Datasets folder.

Now you should be familiar with rest of the steps. We start by importing the libraries:

### 7- Importing Required Libraries

The following code imports required libraries:

```
import pandas as pd
import numpy as np
import matplotlib.pyplot as plt
%matplotlib inline
```

### 8- Importing the Dataset

Execute the following command to import the dataset.

```
iris_data =
pd.read_csv('D:\Datasets\iris
_data.csv')
```

The script above reads the dataset and stores it in *iris_data* dataframe.

### 9- Analyzing the Data

Execute the following script to eyeball the data:

```
iris_data.head()
```

The output looks like this:

|   | sepal_length | sepal_width | petal_length | petal_width | species |
|---|---|---|---|---|---|
| 0 | 5.1 | 3.5 | 1.4 | 0.2 | setosa |
| 1 | 4.9 | 3.0 | 1.4 | 0.2 | setosa |
| 2 | 4.7 | 3.2 | 1.3 | 0.2 | setosa |
| 3 | 4.6 | 3.1 | 1.5 | 0.2 | setosa |
| 4 | 5.0 | 3.6 | 1.4 | 0.2 | setosa |

### 10- Data Preprocessing

To following script divides the data into feature and label set.

```
features = 
player_data.iloc[:, 
0:4].values

labels = player_data.iloc[:, 
4].values
```

Finally let's divide the data into 80 % training and 20% test sets:

```
from sklearn.model_selection 
import train_test_split

train_features, 
test_features, train_labels, 
test_labels = 
train_test_split(features, 
labels, test_size = 0.2, 
random_state = 0)
```

### 11- Scaling the Data

If you look at the dataset it is not scaled well, for instance the petal_width column have values between 0 and 1, while the rest of the columns have higher values. Therefore, before training the algorithm, we will scale our data down. Remember we discussed scaling in the 3rd chapter. Here we will use the standard scalar class.

```
from sklearn.preprocessing
import StandardScaler
feature_scaler =
StandardScaler()
train_features =
feature_scaler.fit_transform(
train_features)
test_features =
feature_scaler.transform(test
_features)
```

## 12- Training the Algorithm and making Predictions

We can see that we have normal distribution for the feature values; therefore we can use Gaussian Naïve Bayes for this problem. To implement Gaussian Naïve Algorithm with Scikit learn we need to use the *GaussianNB* class of the *sklear.naive_bayes* library. Execute the following script to train the model on train_features and train_labels

```
from sklearn.naive_bayes
import GaussianNB
```

```
nb_clf = GaussianNB()
nb_clf.fit(train_features,
train_labels)
```

Execute the following script to predict the label for the test features:

```
predictions = nb_clf.predict(
test_features)
```

To compare predictions with real outputs, execute the following script:

```
comparison=pd.DataFrame({'Rea
l':test_labels,
'Predictions':predictions})
print(comparison)
```

The output looks like this:

|    | Predictions | Real |
|----|-------------|------|
| 0  | virginica   | virginica |
| 1  | versicolor  | versicolor |
| 2  | setosa      | setosa |
| 3  | virginica   | virginica |
| 4  | setosa      | setosa |
| 5  | virginica   | virginica |
| 6  | setosa      | setosa |
| 7  | versicolor  | versicolor |
| 8  | versicolor  | versicolor |
| 9  | versicolor  | versicolor |
| 10 | versicolor  | virginica |
| 11 | versicolor  | versicolor |
| 12 | versicolor  | versicolor |
| 13 | versicolor  | versicolor |
| 14 | versicolor  | versicolor |
| 15 | setosa      | setosa |
| 16 | versicolor  | versicolor |
| 17 | versicolor  | versicolor |
| 18 | setosa      | setosa |
| 19 | setosa      | setosa |
| 20 | virginica   | virginica |
| 21 | versicolor  | versicolor |
| 22 | setosa      | setosa |
| 23 | setosa      | setosa |
| 24 | virginica   | virginica |
| 25 | setosa      | setosa |
| 26 | setosa      | setosa |
| 27 | versicolor  | versicolor |
| 28 | versicolor  | versicolor |
| 29 | setosa      | setosa |

It can be seen from the output that our algorithm did a tremendous job of predicting the flower type. Out of the 30 test instances, 29 have been predicted correctly, while only one (highlighted in red) has been misclassified.

**Evaluating the Algorithm**

To evaluate regression algorithms we used mean absolute error, root mean squared error, and mean squared error. For classification problems the performance metrics are different. Normally Precision, Recall and F1 measures are used to evaluate the performance of classification algorithms. Let's briefly review Confusion Matrix, Accuracy Precision, Recall and F1 Measures are:

Confusion Matrix:

A confusion matrix is a matrix that displays true positive, true negative, false positive and false positive predicted values.

True positives (TP) are those values which are actually positive and they are also predicted positive. Similarly, True Negatives (TN) are those values which are actually negative and predicted negative.

On the other hand, False Positives are the values which are actually negative but have been falsely predicted as positive. Similarly, False Negatives are those which are actually positive but falsely predicted as negative.

A confusion matrix looks like this:

|  | Actual Positive | Actual Negative |
|---|---|---|
| Predicted Positive | True Positive | False Positive |
| Predicted Negative | False Negative | True Negative |

**Accuracy:**

The simplest parameter to evaluate the performance of a machine learning algorithm is Accuracy. Accuracy refers to the number of correctly predicted instance divided the total number of instances. Mathematically it can be represented as:

Accuracy = (TP + TN) / (TP + FP + TN + FN)

### Precision:

Precision refers to the ability of an algorithm to make precise predictions. It can be calculated by dividing the true positives by predicted positives ( true positives + false positives) Mathematically it is represented as:

$$Precision = TP / (TP + FP)$$

### Recall

Recall can be calculated by dividing the true positives by actual number of positives (true positive + false negative)

$$Recall = TP / (TP + FN)$$

### F1 – Measure

F1 measure is the harmonic mean of precision and recall

Like regression performance metrics, we do not have to calculate the values for the aforementioned metrics by hand. Python Scikit Learn library comes with classes that can be used for this purpose. Execute the following script to see the performance of NB algorithm that we trained to predict iris flower type:

```
from sklearn.metrics import classification_report, confusion_matrix, accuracy_score
print(confusion_matrix(test_labels, predictions))
print(classification_report(test_labels, predictions))
print(accuracy_score(test_labels, predictions))
```

The output for the script above looks like this:

```
[[11  0  0]
 [ 0 13  0]
 [ 0  1  5]]
             precision    recall  f1-score   support

     setosa       1.00      1.00      1.00        11
 versicolor       0.93      1.00      0.96        13
  virginica       1.00      0.83      0.91         6

avg / total       0.97      0.97      0.97        30

0.966666666667
```

From the output it can be seen that our algorithm achieved an accuracy of 96.66%.

### *Conclusion*

In this chapter, we started our discussion about the classification algorithms. The first classification algorithm that we studied in this Chapter is the Naïve Bayes Algorithm. We saw the theory behind the algorithm and its implementation with Python.

## Chapter 10

## K Nearest Neighbors Algorithm for Classification

In the last Chapter, we studied Naïve Bayes algorithm for classification. We said that NB algorithm assumes feature independence. Furthermore, one of the drawbacks of the NB algorithm is that it assumes that categorical feature values are normally distributed. However in most of the cases, real world data doesn't follow any trend e.g. uniform distribution or linear separatability etc. In such cases a non-parametric algorithm can come handy. K Nearest Neighbors (KNN) algorithm is one such non-parametric algorithm.

### Theory of KNN

The intuition behind KNN algorithm is extremely simple. KNN algorithm simply finds the distance between the new test data points from all the other data points in the dataset. It then ranks all the other data points in ascending order of their according to their distance with the test point. Finally it chooses the top K nearest data points. It then assigns the new data point to the class of the majority of K data points. Now you should know that why scale our data down so that the distance between the different dimensions of the data points remain distance. Distance can be Manhattan as well as Euclidean depending upon the problem.

Let's visually see the working of a KNN algorithm.

Suppose we have some data points in two dimensional space, divided into two categories: red and blue as shown in the following figure.

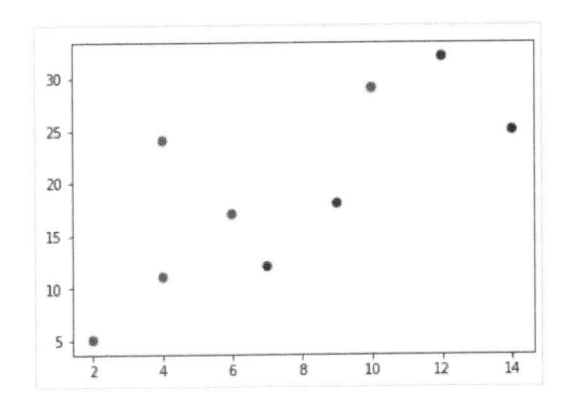

Now if we have to classify a new data point. We will calculate its distance from all the red and blue data points. Then we will choose K nearest data points. Suppose new data point is yellow circle and the value of K is three as shown below:

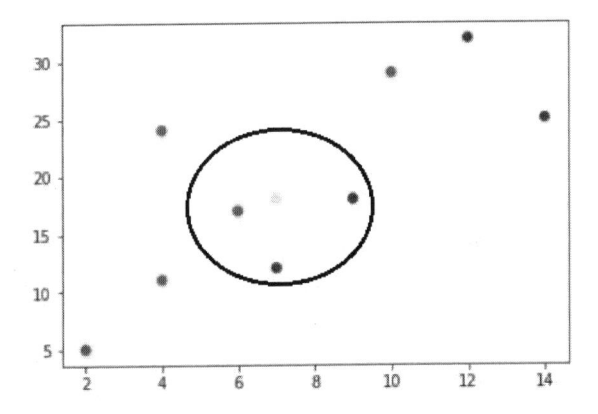

You can see that out of the three nearest neighbors of the yellow data point, two are blue and one is red. Therefore, the yellow data point will be classified in the blue class.

KNN algorithm has no training phase; in fact it uses whole dataset for classifying a new data point. It is for this purpose, it is known as lazy learning algorithm.

## *Advantages of KNN Algorithm*

1. Unlike other algorithms, the list of parameters required by KNN algorithm is not very exhaustive. You only need to specify the number of nearest neighbor K and the type of distance function.

2. KNN algorithm is extremely fast when compared to logistic regression, decision trees and other classification algorithm since there is no training phase involved in KNN. New data point can directly be classified without extensive training, simply by finding its distance from the other data points.

3. KNN is very simple and easy to implement. Furthermore, new data points can be added at any time anytime since whenever a prediction has to be made, distance with all the data points is recalculated.

## *Disadvantages of KNN Algorithm*

1. KNN algorithm work well with numerical features but in case of categorical features, its performance decreases. This is because for categorical features, the distance between two data points cannot be calculated precisely.

2. Prediction cost of KNN algorithm increases with increase in the size of the data and dimensions because it is time consuming to calculate distance between large number of data points with high dimensions.

## *KNN Implementation with Scikit Learn*

In this section we will implement the KNN algorithm with Python's Scikit Learn library. The problem that we are going to solve with KNN algorithm is predicting whether a bank currency note is genuine or not. We have four attributes in the dataset i.e. entropy, skewness, variance and curtosis of the wavelet transformed image of the currency note.

More details about the dataset can be found at this link.

The dataset has been supplied with the book and can be found by the name of banknote_data.csv in the Datasets folder.

As always we start by importing the libraries:

### 13- Importing Required Libraries

The following code imports required libraries:

```
import pandas as pd
import numpy as np
```

```
import matplotlib.pyplot as plt
%matplotlib inline
```

### 14- Importing the Dataset

Execute the following command to import the dataset.

```
banknote_data = pd.read_csv(r'D:\Datasets\banknote_data.csv')
```

The script above reads the dataset and stores it in *banknote_data dataframe*.

### 15- Analyzing the Data

The following script returns the data dimensions:

```
banknote_data.shape
```

The above script returns (1372, 5) which means that our dataset contains 1372 records and five attributes.

Execute the following script to eyeball the data:

```
banknote_data.head()
```

The output looks like this:

|   | Variance | Skewness | Curtosis | Entropy | Class |
|---|----------|----------|----------|---------|-------|
| 0 | 3.62160  | 8.6661   | -2.8073  | -0.44699 | 0 |
| 1 | 4.54590  | 8.1674   | -2.4586  | -1.46210 | 0 |
| 2 | 3.86600  | -2.6383  | 1.9242   | 0.10645  | 0 |
| 3 | 3.45660  | 9.5228   | -4.0112  | -3.59440 | 0 |
| 4 | 0.32924  | -4.4552  | 4.5718   | -0.98880 | 0 |

## 16- Data Preprocessing

To following script divides the data into feature and label set.

```
features= banknote_data.iloc[:,0:4].values
labels= banknote_data.iloc[:,4].values
```

Finally let's divide the data into 80 % training and 20% test sets:

```
from sklearn.model_selection import train_test_split
train_features, test_features, train_labels, test_labels =
```

```
train_test_split(features,
labels, test_size = 0.2,
random_state = 0)
```

### 17- Scaling the Data

If you are using KNN algorithm, it is always a good practice to scale your data. Remember we discussed scaling in the 3rd chapter. Here we will use the standard scalar class.

```
from sklearn.preprocessing
import StandardScaler

feature_scaler =
StandardScaler()

train_features =
feature_scaler.fit_transform(
train_features)

test_features =
feature_scaler.transform(test
_features)
```

### 18- Training the Algorithm and making Predictions

To implement KNN Algorithm with Scikit learn we need to use the

*KNeighborsClassifier* class of the *sklear.neighbors* library. The value of K is specified as value for the *n_neighbors* parameter as shown in the following script. We use a value of 3 for K. Execute the following script to train the model on train_features and train_labels

```
from sklearn.neighbors import KNeighborsClassifier
knn_clf = KNeighborsClassifier(n_neighbors=3)
knn_clf.fit(train_features, train_labels)
```

Execute the following script to predict the label for the test features:

```
predictions = nb_clf.predict(test_features)
```

To compare predictions with real outputs, execute the following script:

```
comparison=pd.DataFrame({'Real':test_labels,
'Predictions':predictions})
```

```
print(comparison)
```

The output looks like this:

|    | Predictions | Real |
|----|-------------|------|
| 0  | 1 | 1 |
| 1  | 0 | 0 |
| 2  | 1 | 1 |
| 3  | 0 | 0 |
| 4  | 0 | 0 |
| 5  | 0 | 0 |
| 6  | 0 | 0 |
| 7  | 0 | 0 |
| 8  | 1 | 1 |
| 9  | 1 | 1 |
| 10 | 0 | 0 |
| 11 | 0 | 0 |
| 12 | 1 | 1 |
| 13 | 0 | 0 |
| 14 | 0 | 0 |
| 15 | 0 | 0 |
| 16 | 1 | 1 |
| 17 | 1 | 1 |
| 18 | 0 | 0 |
| 19 | 0 | 0 |
| 20 | 1 | 1 |
| 21 | 0 | 0 |
| 22 | 0 | 0 |
| 23 | 1 | 1 |
| 24 | 0 | 0 |
| 25 | 1 | 1 |
| 26 | 0 | 0 |
| 27 | 1 | 1 |

You can see that most of our predictions are accurate.

## Evaluating the Algorithm

From the last chapter, we know that to evaluate performance of classification algorithms we can use confusion matrix, accuracy, precision, and recall and F1 measure as metrics. Execute the following script to find the values for these metrics:

```
from sklearn.metrics import classification_report, confusion_matrix, accuracy_score
print(confusion_matrix(test_labels, predictions))
print(classification_report(test_labels, predictions))
print(accuracy_score(test_labels, predictions))
```

The output of the script above looks like this:

```
[[157   0]
 [  0 118]]
             precision    recall  f1-score   support

          0       1.00      1.00      1.00       157
          1       1.00      1.00      1.00       118

avg / total       1.00      1.00      1.00       275

1.0
```

It can be seen from the output that our algorithm did a pretty good job at predicting the authenticity of bank note. We got 100% accuracy.

## *Effect of Value of K on Prediction Accuracy*

In the previous section, we randomly set the value of K to 3 which incidentally resulted in 100% accuracy. However, this is not always the case. We don't know the best value of K from the outset. The best way to find the value of K is to try different values of K and choose the value that result in highest accuracy.

In the script below will again predict the authentication of currency note by using values of k between 1 and 50. Execute the following script:

```
rate_of_error = []


for i in range(1, 50):
```

```python
    knn = KNeighborsClassifier(n_neighbors=i)
    knn.fit(train_features, train_labels)
    predictions = knn.predict(test_features)

rate_of_error.append(np.mean(predictions != test_labels))
```

Once errors are calculated per value of K, a chart can be printed showing the error rates with change in value of K. Execute the following script:

```python
plt.figure(figsize=(10, 5))
plt.plot(range(1, 50), rate_of_error, color='green', linestyle='solid', marker='o',
markerfacecolor='red', markersize=10)
plt.title('K value vs Error')
plt.xlabel('K Value')
plt.ylabel('Error Value')
```

The output looks like this:

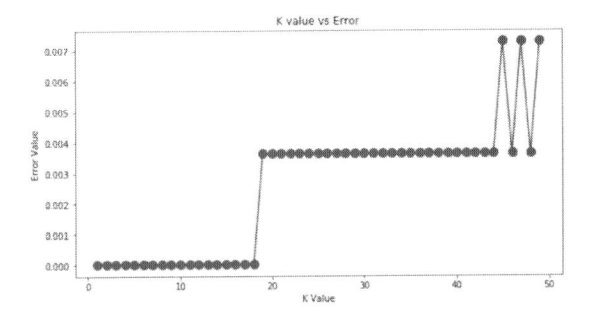

From the above picture, it is clear that the error remains at zero for all the values of K between 1 and 18. After 18, the error increases to 4% which still not huge.

## *Conclusion*

In this chapter, we covered K Nearest Neighbor algorithm for classification. We studied the theory behind K Nearest Neighbors algorithm and then implemented the algorithm to solve the problem of bank note authentication. In the next chapter we will see how we can use Decision Tree algorithm for classification Tasks.

## *Chapter 11*

## *Decision Tree for Classification*

In chapter 6, "Decision Tree for Regression" we studied how a decision tree works and what are the steps involved in the decision making process of a decision tree. However, in Chapter 6 we used decision tree for regression tasks i.e. for predicting petrol prices. In addition to regression, we can also use decision tree for classification tasks. This is what we are going to do in this chapter. This chapter will be fairly brief since we have covered decision tree in detail in Chapter 6. Here we will just see an example of how decision tree solves classification problem with the help of Python's Scikit Learn Library.

# *Solving Classification Problems with Decision Tree in Python Scikit Learn*

In Chapter 9, we predicted the type of Iris flower using Naïve Bayes Algorithm. Let's try to solve the same classification task with the help of decision tree algorithm.

We start by importing the libraries:

### 1- Importing Required Libraries

The following code imports required libraries:

```
import pandas as pd
import numpy as np
import matplotlib.pyplot as plt
%matplotlib inline
```

### 2- Importing the Dataset

Execute the following command to import the dataset.

```
iris_data = pd.read_csv('D:\Datasets\iris_data.csv')
```

The script above reads the dataset and stores it in *iris_data dataframe*.

### 3- Analyzing the Data

Execute the following script to eyeball the data:

```
iris_data.head()
```

The output looks like this:

|   | sepal_length | sepal_width | petal_length | petal_width | species |
|---|---|---|---|---|---|
| 0 | 5.1 | 3.5 | 1.4 | 0.2 | setosa |
| 1 | 4.9 | 3.0 | 1.4 | 0.2 | setosa |
| 2 | 4.7 | 3.2 | 1.3 | 0.2 | setosa |
| 3 | 4.6 | 3.1 | 1.5 | 0.2 | setosa |
| 4 | 5.0 | 3.6 | 1.4 | 0.2 | setosa |

### 4- Data Preprocessing

To following script divides the data into feature and label set.

```
features = iris_data.iloc[:, 0:4].values
labels = iris_data.iloc[:, 4].values
```

Finally let's divide the data into 80 % training and 20% test sets:

```
from sklearn.model_selection
import train_test_split

train_features,
test_features, train_labels,
test_labels =
train_test_split(features,
labels, test_size = 0.2,
random_state = 0)
```

### 5- Scaling the Data

If you look at the dataset it is not scaled well, for instance the petal_width column have values between 0 and 1, while the rest of the columns have higher values. Therefore, before training the algorithm, we will scale our data down. Remember we discussed scaling in the 3rd chapter. Here we will use the standard scalar class.

```
from sklearn.preprocessing
import StandardScaler

feature_scaler =
StandardScaler()

train_features =
feature_scaler.fit_transform(
train_features)
```

```
test_features =
feature_scaler.transform(test
_features)
```

## 6- Training the Algorithm and making Predictions

We can see that we have normal distribution for the feature values; therefore we can use Gaussian Naïve Bayes for this problem. To implement Gaussian Naïve Algorithm with Scikit learn we need to use the *DecisionTreeClassifier* class of the *sklear.tree* library. Execute the following script to train the model on train_features and train_labels

```
from sklearn.tree import DecisionTreeClassifier
dt_clf = DecisionTreeClassifier(random_state=0)
dt_clf.fit(train_features, train_labels)
```

Execute the following script to predict the label for the test features:

```
predictions = dt_clf.predict(test_features)
```

To compare predictions with real outputs, execute the following script:

```
comparison=pd.DataFrame({'Real':test_labels,
'Predictions':predictions})
print(comparison)
```

The output looks like this:

|    | Predictions | Real |
|----|-------------|------|
| 0  | virginica   | virginica |
| 1  | versicolor  | versicolor |
| 2  | setosa      | setosa |
| 3  | virginica   | virginica |
| 4  | setosa      | setosa |
| 5  | virginica   | virginica |
| 6  | setosa      | setosa |
| 7  | versicolor  | versicolor |
| 8  | versicolor  | versicolor |
| 9  | versicolor  | versicolor |
| 10 | virginica   | virginica |
| 11 | versicolor  | versicolor |
| 12 | versicolor  | versicolor |
| 13 | versicolor  | versicolor |
| 14 | versicolor  | versicolor |
| 15 | setosa      | setosa |
| 16 | versicolor  | versicolor |
| 17 | versicolor  | versicolor |
| 18 | setosa      | setosa |
| 19 | setosa      | setosa |
| 20 | virginica   | virginica |
| 21 | versicolor  | versicolor |
| 22 | setosa      | setosa |
| 23 | setosa      | setosa |
| 24 | virginica   | virginica |
| 25 | setosa      | setosa |
| 26 | setosa      | setosa |
| 27 | versicolor  | versicolor |
| 28 | versicolor  | versicolor |

## Evaluating the Algorithm

The following script returns values for performance metrics of our classification algorithm:

```
from sklearn.metrics import classification_report,
```

```
confusion_matrix,
accuracy_score
print(confusion_matrix(test_l
abels, predictions))
print(classification_report(t
est_labels, predictions))
print(accuracy_score(test_lab
els, predictions))
```

The output looks like this:

```
[[11  0  0]
 [ 0 13  0]
 [ 0  0  6]]
             precision    recall  f1-score   support

     setosa       1.00      1.00      1.00        11
 versicolor       1.00      1.00      1.00        13
  virginica       1.00      1.00      1.00         6

avg / total       1.00      1.00      1.00        30

1.0
```

From the output it can be seen that 100% prediction accuracy has been achieved using decision tree algorithm which is greater than 96.66% achieved using Naïve Bayes algorithm in Chapter 9

***Conclusion***

In this chapter we studied how decision tree algorithm can be used for classification tasks. In the next chapter we will study how random forest algorithm can also be used to perform classification tasks.

## Chapter 12

## Random Forest for Classification

In chapter 7, we studied the details of Random Forest Algorithm and saw its pros and cons. We also implemented Random Forest algorithm in Python Scikit Learn to solve regression problem. However, we can also use Random Forest algorithm for classification problems. Since we are in classification section, it makes sense to add a chapter dedicated to Random Forest algorithm for classification.

We will not go into the theory of Random Forest algorithm here since it has already been covered in Chapter 7. We will straight jump into the code section. As always we will use Python's Scikit Learn Library to implement Random Forest Algorithm for classification.

## *Implementing Random Forest Classification with Python's Scikit Learn*

The problem that we are going to solve with Random Forest algorithm is predicting whether a bank currency note is genuine or not. This is the same problem that we solved in Chapter 10 (KNN Algorithm). We have four attributes in the dataset i.e. entropy, skew-ness, variance and curtosis of the wavelet transformed image of the currency note.

More details about the dataset can be found at this link.

The dataset has been supplied with the book and can be found by the name of banknote_data.csv in the Datasets folder. Follow these steps

   **1- Importing Required Libraries**

```
import pandas as pd
import numpy as np
import matplotlib.pyplot as plt
%matplotlib inline
```

## 2- Importing the Dataset

The following script imports the dataset.

```
banknote_data = pd.read_csv(r'D:\Datasets\banknote_data.csv')
```

The script above reads the dataset and stores it in *banknote_data dataframe*.

## 3- Analyzing the Data

The following script returns the data dimensions:

```
banknote_data.shape
```

The above script returns (1372, 5) which means that our dataset contains 1372 records and five attributes.

To see how the data looks like, execute the following script. It returns the first five rows of the data.

```
banknote_data.head()
```

The output looks like this:

|   | Variance | Skewness | Curtosis | Entropy | Class |
|---|---|---|---|---|---|
| 0 | 3.62160 | 8.6661 | -2.8073 | -0.44699 | 0 |
| 1 | 4.54590 | 8.1674 | -2.4586 | -1.46210 | 0 |
| 2 | 3.86600 | -2.6383 | 1.9242 | 0.10645 | 0 |
| 3 | 3.45660 | 9.5228 | -4.0112 | -3.59440 | 0 |
| 4 | 0.32924 | -4.4552 | 4.5718 | -0.98880 | 0 |

### 4- Data Preprocessing

To following script divides the data into feature and label set.

```
features=
banknote_data.iloc[:,0:4].val
ues
labels=
banknote_data.iloc[:,4].value
s
```

Finally let's divide the data into 80 % training and 20% test sets:

```
from sklearn.model_selection
import train_test_split

train_features,
test_features, train_labels,
test_labels =
train_test_split(features,
labels, test_size = 0.2,
random_state = 0)
```

### 5- Scaling the Data

For Random Forest algorithm, it is not necessary to scale the data, however just for the sake of practice, let's scale the data using standard scalar. Remember we discussed scaling in the 3rd chapter.

```
from sklearn.preprocessing
import StandardScaler

feature_scaler =
StandardScaler()

train_features =
feature_scaler.fit_transform(
train_features)

test_features =
feature_scaler.transform(test
_features)
```

## 6- Training the Algorithm and making Predictions

To solve regression problems with Random Forest, we can use *RandomForestRegressor* class of the *sklearn.ensemble* library. For classification problems we need to use *RandomForestClassifier* class of the same library. Execute the following script to train the model on train_features and train_labels.

```
from sklearn.ensemble import RandomForestClassifier

rf_clf = RandomForestClassifier(n_estimators=50, random_state=0)
rf_clf.fit(train_features, train_labels)
```

Execute the following script to predict the label for the test features:

```
predictions = rf_clf .predict( test_features)
```

To compare predictions with real outputs, execute the following script:

```
comparison=pd.DataFrame({'Rea
l':test_labels,
'Predictions':predictions})
print(comparison)
```

A snippet of the output looks like this:

|    | Predictions | Real |
|----|-------------|------|
| 0  | 1 | 1 |
| 1  | 0 | 0 |
| 2  | 1 | 1 |
| 3  | 0 | 0 |
| 4  | 0 | 0 |
| 5  | 0 | 0 |
| 6  | 0 | 0 |
| 7  | 0 | 0 |
| 8  | 1 | 1 |
| 9  | 1 | 1 |
| 10 | 0 | 0 |
| 11 | 0 | 0 |
| 12 | 1 | 1 |
| 13 | 0 | 0 |
| 14 | 0 | 0 |
| 15 | 0 | 0 |
| 16 | 1 | 1 |
| 17 | 1 | 1 |
| 18 | 0 | 0 |
| 19 | 0 | 0 |
| 20 | 1 | 1 |
| 21 | 0 | 0 |
| 22 | 0 | 0 |
| 23 | 1 | 1 |
| 24 | 0 | 0 |
| 25 | 1 | 1 |
| 26 | 0 | 0 |

## 7- Evaluating the Algorithm

We know that to evaluate performance of classification algorithms we can use confusion matrix, accuracy, precision, and recall and F1 measure as metrics. Execute the following script to find the values for these metrics:

```
from sklearn.metrics import classification_report, confusion_matrix, accuracy_score
print(confusion_matrix(test_labels, predictions))
print(classification_report(test_labels, predictions))
print(accuracy_score(test_labels, predictions))
```

The output of the script above looks like this:

```
[[155   2]
 [  1 117]]
             precision    recall  f1-score   support

          0       0.99      0.99      0.99       157
          1       0.98      0.99      0.99       118

avg / total       0.99      0.99      0.99       275

0.989090909091
```

From the above output it can be seen that we have three wrong predictions in case of Random Forest classification. For KNN we had zero wrong predictions. Try to change the value for the number of estimators and see if you can get better results with Random Forest algorithm or not.

## *Conclusion*

In this Chapter we saw how Random Forest algorithm can be used to solve classification problem. In the next chapter, we will see how Support Vector Machines algorithm can be used to solve classification problems.

## Chapter 13

## Support Vector Machines for Classification

In Chapter 8, we studied Support Vector Regression algorithm which is a variant of Support Vector Machines (SVM) algorithm and is used to solve regression problems. We studied the theory of SVM algorithm and also saw what are the pros and cons of SVM algorithm in Chapter 8 in detail. In this Chapter we will see how SVM algorithm can be used to solve classification problems. We will not focus on theoretical details of SVM in this Chapter since they have already been covered in Chapter 8. Here we will see how we can implement SVM algorithm in Python to solve classification problem.

# *SVM for classification using Python's Scikit Learn*

In Chapter 9 and 11, we predicted the type of Iris flower using Naïve Bayes Algorithm and Decision Trees algorithm, respectively. Let's try to solve the same classification task with the help of Support Vector Machines algorithm.

We start by importing the libraries:

### 1- Importing Required Libraries

The following code imports required libraries:

```
import pandas as pd
import numpy as np
import matplotlib.pyplot as plt
%matplotlib inline
```

### 2- Importing the Dataset

Execute the following command to import the dataset.

```
iris_data = 
pd.read_csv('D:\Datasets\iris
_data.csv')
```

The script above reads the dataset and stores it in *iris_data dataframe*.

### 3- Analyzing the Data

Execute the following script to eyeball the data:

```
iris_data.head()
```

The output looks like this:

|   | sepal_length | sepal_width | petal_length | petal_width | species |
|---|---|---|---|---|---|
| 0 | 5.1 | 3.5 | 1.4 | 0.2 | setosa |
| 1 | 4.9 | 3.0 | 1.4 | 0.2 | setosa |
| 2 | 4.7 | 3.2 | 1.3 | 0.2 | setosa |
| 3 | 4.6 | 3.1 | 1.5 | 0.2 | setosa |
| 4 | 5.0 | 3.6 | 1.4 | 0.2 | setosa |

### 4- Data Preprocessing

To following script divides the data into feature and label set.

```
features = iris_data.iloc[:,
0:4].values

labels = iris_data.iloc[:,
4].values
```

Finally let's divide the data into 80 % training and 20% test sets:

```
from sklearn.model_selection import train_test_split
train_features, test_features, train_labels, test_labels = train_test_split(features, labels, test_size = 0.2, random_state = 0)
```

### 5- Scaling the Data

If you look at the dataset it is not scaled well, for instance the petal_width column have values between 0 and 1, while the rest of the columns have higher values. Therefore, before training the algorithm, we will scale our data down.

```
from sklearn.preprocessing import StandardScaler
feature_scaler = StandardScaler()
train_features = feature_scaler.fit_transform(train_features)
```

```
test_features =
feature_scaler.transform(test
_features)
```

## 6- Training the Algorithm and making Predictions

In case of regression we used *SVR* class of the *sklearn.svm* library. For classification we need to use *SVC* class of the same library. Execute the following script to train the model on train_features and train_labels

```
from sklearn.svm import SVC
svm_clf = SVC()
svm_clf.fit(train_features,
train_labels)
```

Execute the following script to predict the label for the test features:

```
predictions =
svm_clf.fit.predict(
test_features)
```

To compare predictions with real outputs, execute the following script:

```
comparison=pd.DataFrame({'Real':test_labels,
'Predictions':predictions})
print(comparison)
```

The output looks like this:

|    | Predictions | Real       |
|----|-------------|------------|
| 0  | virginica   | virginica  |
| 1  | versicolor  | versicolor |
| 2  | setosa      | setosa     |
| 3  | virginica   | virginica  |
| 4  | setosa      | setosa     |
| 5  | virginica   | virginica  |
| 6  | setosa      | setosa     |
| 7  | versicolor  | versicolor |
| 8  | versicolor  | versicolor |
| 9  | versicolor  | versicolor |
| 10 | virginica   | virginica  |
| 11 | versicolor  | versicolor |
| 12 | versicolor  | versicolor |
| 13 | versicolor  | versicolor |
| 14 | versicolor  | versicolor |
| 15 | setosa      | setosa     |
| 16 | versicolor  | versicolor |
| 17 | versicolor  | versicolor |
| 18 | setosa      | setosa     |
| 19 | setosa      | setosa     |
| 20 | virginica   | virginica  |
| 21 | versicolor  | versicolor |
| 22 | setosa      | setosa     |
| 23 | setosa      | setosa     |
| 24 | virginica   | virginica  |
| 25 | setosa      | setosa     |
| 26 | setosa      | setosa     |
| 27 | versicolor  | versicolor |
| 28 | versicolor  | versicolor |

## Evaluating the Algorithm

The following script returns values for performance metrics of our classification algorithm:

```
from sklearn.metrics import classification_report,
```

```
confusion_matrix,
accuracy_score

print(confusion_matrix(test_l
abels, predictions))

print(classification_report(t
est_labels, predictions))

print(accuracy_score(test_lab
els, predictions))
```

The output looks like this:

```
[[11  0  0]
 [ 0 13  0]
 [ 0  0  6]]
              precision    recall  f1-score   support

     setosa        1.00      1.00      1.00        11
 versicolor        1.00      1.00      1.00        13
  virginica        1.00      1.00      1.00         6

avg / total        1.00      1.00      1.00        30

1.0
```

From the output it can be seen that 100% prediction accuracy has been achieved using decision tree algorithm which is greater than 96.66% achieved using Naïve Bayes algorithm in Chapter 9 and is equal to the accuracy achieved using Decision Tree classification algorithm in Chapter 11.

**Conclusion**

With this section we are going to end the Classification section of our supervised machine learning Part of the book. In the next chapter we will start studying unsupervised machine learning. In unsupervised machine learning we will study two clustering algorithms i.e. K-Means Clustering and Hierarchical Clustering. Happy Coding!!!

## Chapter 14

## K Means Clustering Algorithm

In the previous chapters we covered Supervised Machine Learning. We saw Regression and Classification that are the two main types of Supervised Learning. In this chapter and the next, we will cover Unsupervised Machine Learning i.e. learning from unlabeled data. In this Chapter we will study K-Means clustering algorithm.

K Means algorithm is one of the most widely used unsupervised machine learning algorithm used for clustering data points based on their similarity measure.

## Steps of K-Mean Clustering

K-Means clustering algorithm is extremely simple and easy to understand. Following are the steps involved in K-Means clustering:

1- Randomly choose the number of centroids K. Where K corresponds to the number of clusters that you want your data grouped to.
2- Find the distance between all the data points and all the centroids. The distance can be Euclidean or Manhattan but normally Euclidean distance is used.
3- Assign the data points to the centroid with least distance. Repeat this step for all the data points forming K clusters of points.
4- Update the location of each centroid by taking mean of x and y components of all the points in the cluster.
5- Repeat steps 2, 3 and 4 until updated positions of all the centroids are same as their previous positions.

Luckily for us, we don't have to perform all these steps manually. We can simply use Python's Scikit Learn library for clustering tasks as well.

## *K-Means Clustering With Python's Scikit Learn*

In Chapter 4, Regression, we predicted the price of cars based on their year of manufacturing. In this section we will see how we cluster those cars into different clusters based on similarities. So let's start clustering.

1. **Importing Libraries**

As always, the first step is to import required libraries:

```
import pandas as pd
import numpy as np
import matplotlib.pyplot as plt
%matplotlib inline
```

## 2. Importing Data

The following script imports the data:

```
car_data = pd.read_csv('D:\Datasets\car_price.csv')
```

## 3. Data Analysis

Execute the following script to see how our dataset looks like:

```
car_data.head()
```

The output looks like this:

|   | Year | Price |
|---|------|-------|
| 0 | 1980 | 2000  |
| 1 | 1985 | 3000  |
| 2 | 1983 | 2200  |
| 3 | 1990 | 3700  |
| 4 | 1995 | 4500  |

Finally, lets plot the data and see if can find any clusters in the dataset. Execute the following script:

```
plt.scatter(car_data['Year'],
car_data['Price'])
plt.title("Year vs Price")
plt.xlabel("Year")
plt.ylabel("Price")
plt.show()
```

The output of the script above looks like this:

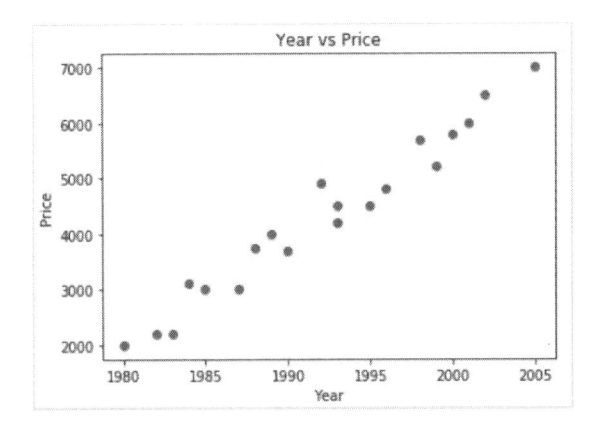

If we look at the above graph we do not find any visible clusters. However if we are tasked with dividing the above data points into three clusters, we might form a cluster of cars with low price and very old models (points at the bottom left), a cluster of cars with medium price and old models (points in the middle of the chart) and a cluster of cars that are relatively new and have higher prices (points at the top right). Let's try to divide the above data points into three clusters using Python's Sklearn Library.

### 4. Clustering the Data

To implement K-Means clustering with sklearn, the *KMeans* class of the *sklearn.cluster* library is used. The number of clusters can be defined by *n_cluster* parameter of *KMeans* class. In the script below, we create three clusters. The *fit* method is then called to cluster the data as shown in the following script:

```
from sklearn.cluster import KMeans
km_clus = KMeans(n_clusters=3)
km_clus.fit(car_data)
```

Now to find the centroids found by our clustering algorithm we can use the *cluster_centers_* attribute of the KMeans object as shown below:

```
print(km_clus.cluster_centers
_)
```

The output looks like this:

```
[[ 1992.77777778   4394.44444444]
 [ 1983.5          2583.33333333]
 [ 2001.2          6200.        ]]
```

These are the coordinates of the centroids of the three clusters formed by the KMeans clustering algorithm for car_price data.

To find the labels of the different data points, use the labels_ attribute as shown below:

```
print(km_clus.labels_)
```

The output looks like this:

```
[1 1 1 0 0 2 1 2 0 0 1 0 0 2 2 0 0 2 0 1]
```

The three clusters formed by the algorithm have been named 0, 1 and 2. It is important to mention that these cluster names have no mathematical significance and they are there just to name the clusters. If there was another cluster, it would have been labeled as 4.

### 5. Plotting the Clusters

The labels don't given any visual information about the clusters. Therefore, let's plot clusters. Execute the following script:

```
plt.scatter(car_data['Year'],
car_data['Price'],          c          =
km_clus.labels_,
cmap='rainbow')
```

The output looks like this:

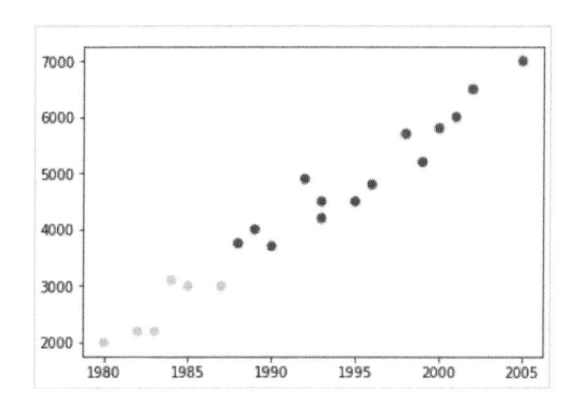

From the output we can see that the clusters formed are according to our expectations. Cars with low price and very old manufacturing year have been clustered together in the(green data points, cars that are average old and have average price have been clustered together (blue data points) and cars with new models and high price have been clustered together (red data points)

Finally, let's see the centroid along with clusters, execute the following script:

```
plt.scatter(car_data['Year'],
car_data['Price'], c =
km_clus.labels_,
cmap='rainbow')
plt.scatter(km_clus.cluster_c
enters_[:,0],km_clus.cluster_
centers_[:,1],
color='yellow')
```

The output looks like this:

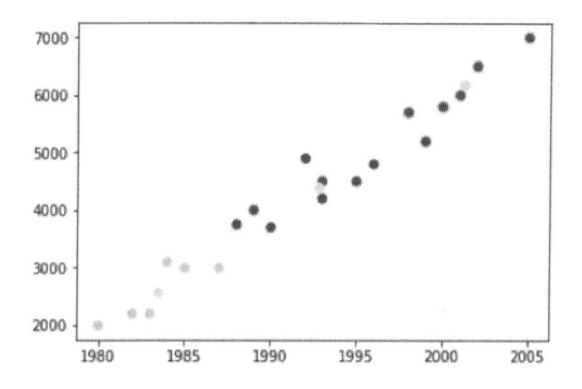

The centroids for each cluster have been displayed in yellow.

***Conclusion***

In this chapter, we studied a very interesting clustering technique i.e. K-Means clustering. In the next chapter we will study another extremely useful clustering technique i.e. Hierarchical Clustering!

## Chapter 15

## *Hierarchical Clustering*

In the last chapter we studied K-Mean clustering which is a type of unsupervised learning. In this chapter we are going to study another clustering technique i.e. Hierarchical Clustering. Clustered formed by hierarchical clustering, can be sometimes similar to the K-Means clustering; however the process of Hierarchical Clustering is quite different. Hierarchical Clustering has two types: Divisive and Agglomerative. In divisive clustering, the data points are initially treated as one big cluster and a top-down approach is followed to divide this one big cluster into several small clusters. On the other hand in Agglomerative clustering involves bottom-up approach. In this chapter, we will cover Agglomerative clustering since it is the most commonly used clustering type.

## *Hierarchical Clustering Theory*

Hierarchical clustering involves following steps:

1. In the beginning every data point is treated as one cluster. Therefore, if there are N data points the total number of clusters at the beginning are N.
2. Join the two closest points, resulting in N-1 clusters.
3. Again join the two closest clusters from to form N-2 clusters.
4. Repeat step 3 until one huge cluster is formed.
5. Use dendrograms to divide one big cluster into required number of clusters. We will study the concept of dendrograms in details

**Calculating Cluster Distance**

It is important to mention here that there are several ways to find distance between the two clusters and both Euclidean and Manhattan distances can be used for this purpose. Distance between the clusters can be calculated using one of the following ways:

1. Distance between two closest points of the cluster can be calculated.
2. Distance between two farthest points of the cluster can be calculated.
3. Distance between the centroids of two clusters can be calculated.
4. Mean of the distance between all possible combinations of points can be calculated.

## Using Dendrograms for Clustering

We said earlier that dendrograms are used to divide one huge cluster into required number of clusters. In this section we will see with the help of an example as to how dendrograms actually work.

Execute the following script:

```
import numpy as np

data = np.array([
    [1992,3000],
    [1995,4000],
    [1998,4500],
    [1996,4200],
    [1999,4700],
    [1993,3500],
    [2001,5700],
    [2004,6000],
    [2008,6500],
    [2005,5800],
    [2007,6200],
    [2009,6700],])
```

The script above creates a two dimensional list of integers. Consider them car models and corresponding price.

Let's plot these data points. Execute the following script to do so:

```python
import matplotlib.pyplot as plt

annots = range(1, 13)
plt.figure(figsize=(12, 8))
plt.subplots_adjust(bottom=0.1)
plt.scatter(data[:,0],data[:,1], label='True Position')

for label, x, y in zip(annots, data[:, 0], data[:, 1]):
    plt.annotate(
        label,
        xy=(x, y), xytext=(-2, 2),
        textcoords='offset points', ha='right', va='bottom')
plt.show()
```

The data points look like this:

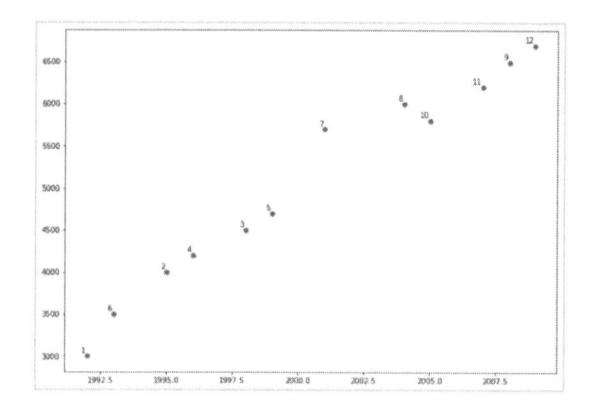

From the first look we can see that point's 1-6 form one cluster and points 7 to 12 form another cluster.

Now let's see how dendrograms are used to form these clusters. Execute the following script to create dendrograms for the above data points.

```
from scipy.cluster.hierarchy import dendrogram, linkage
from matplotlib import pyplot as plt


annot = linkage(data, 'single')
```

```
marks = range(1, 13)

plt.figure(figsize=(12, 8))
dendrogram(annot,
orientation='top',
           labels=marks,
distance_sort='descending',
show_leaf_counts=True)
plt.show()
```

To create the dendrograms we can use the *dendrogram* and *linkage* classes of the *scipy.cluster.hierarchy* library.

The dendrograms generated for the above data points looks like this:

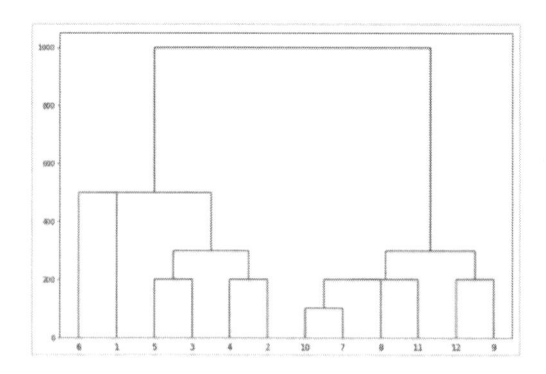

Dendrograms are created following the steps we mentioned earlier. First the two closest points are joined together. These points are depicted at the bottom of the dendrogram hierarchy. For instance points 6 and 1, 5 and 3, 4 and 2, 10 and 7, these points are closest to each other. The vertical height of the point corresponds to Euclidean distance between the points. Finally when the closes points are joined to form clusters, the closest clusters are joined together, for instance cluster of points 5, 3 and 3, 4 have been joined together. This process continues until one big cluster is formed.

Once one large cluster is formed, find longest vertical line with no horizontal line passing through it. Draw a horizontal line through. The number of points at which the horizontal line cross vertical lines, will be the number of clusters.

For instance in the following figure, the dotted black line is the vertical line with longest distance. We drew a red line through this vertical line. The red line cuts two vertical lines resulting in two clusters as shown below:

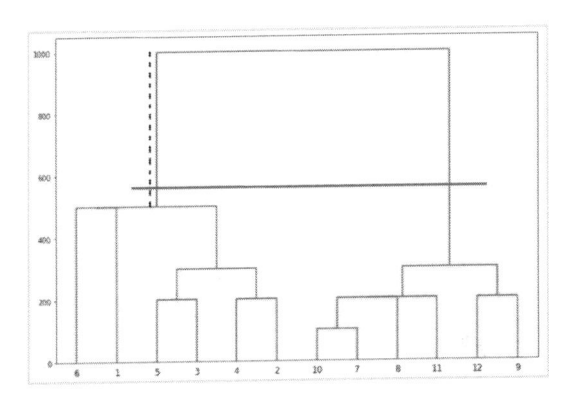

If you look at the points in two clusters, green cluster contains points 1 to 6 while red cluster contains points 7 to 12 as expected.

## *Hierarchical Clustering with Python Scikit Learn*

In the last section we draw dendrograms using Scipy library. However hierarchical clustering can also be implemented using Python's Scikit Learn Library.

The problem that we are going to solve in this section is to cluster the customers into groups based on their spending habits. The data has been downloaded and named as customer_records.csv.

Next, follow these steps to implement hierarchical clustering with Python Scikit Learn:

**Importing Libraries**

```
import matplotlib.pyplot as plt
import pandas as pd
import numpy as np
```

```
%matplotlib inline
```

## Importing the Dataset

The following script imports the dataset and stores it in customer_record dataframe

```
customer_record =
pd.read_csv('D:\Datasets\cust
omer_records.csv')
```

To view the dataset, execute the following script:

```
customer_record.head()
```

The output looks like this:

| | CustomerID | Genre | Age | Annual Income (k$) | Spending Score (1-100) |
|---|---|---|---|---|---|
| 0 | 1 | Male | 19 | 15 | 39 |
| 1 | 2 | Male | 21 | 15 | 81 |
| 2 | 3 | Female | 20 | 16 | 6 |
| 3 | 4 | Female | 23 | 16 | 77 |
| 4 | 5 | Female | 31 | 17 | 40 |

The dataset has five attributes CustomerID, Genre, Age, Annual Income (In thousand dollars) and Spending Score (1-100). The spending score column corresponds to user spending habits. The more a user spends, the higher is this spending score column. For the sake of simplicity, we will just take two columns i.e. Annual Income and Spending Score and try to cluster our data according to these two columns. To select the two columns, execute the following script:

```
dataset = customer_record.iloc[:, 3:5].values
```

## Clustering the Data

To cluster the data using Python's Scikit Learn, we can use the *scipy.cluster.hierarchy* library. It has two classes: *linkage* and *dendrogram*. First we need to create an object of linkage class and pass the dataset and the distance method to linkage class. Next we need to pass the object of the linkage class to dendrogram class as shown in the following script. Here the distance method used is "ward" which basically minimizes the distance variants between multiple clusters. Execute the following script:

```
import scipy.cluster.hierarchy as hc

plt.figure(figsize=(12, 8))
plt.title("Customer Clusters")
link = hc.linkage(dataset, method='ward')
dendograms = hc.dendrogram(link)
```

The above script results in the following dendogram chart:

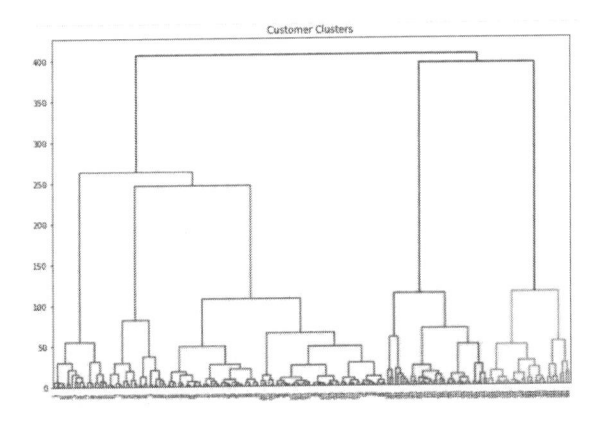

In the above script let's draw a line at 200 at vertical axis. This will give us five clusters as shown in the following figure:

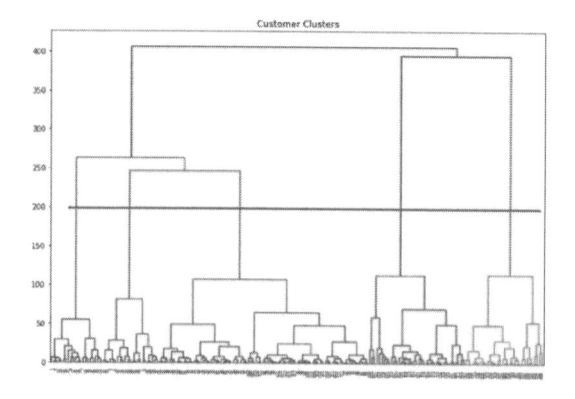

Similarly if you draw horizontal line at 300, the resulting number of cluster will be 3. Higher threshold results in lesser number of clusters and vice versa.

***Conclusion***

In this Chapter we studied Hierarchical Clustering which is a very important unsupervised learning technique. With this we will end the unsupervised learning section. In the next Chapter we will study dimensionality reduction techniques i.e. Principal component analysis and Linear Discriminant analysis. Happy Coding!!!

## Chapter 16

## Dimensionality Reduction with PCA

Machine learning as a discipline has advanced quite a bit in recent years owing to the availability of high performance hardware and storage spaces. Algorithms that use to take months to run 20 years ago can now be run in minutes. Though execution speed of machine learning algorithms has improved significantly, there are still few bottlenecks that slow machine learning algorithms down.

Huge dataset and large number of features per dataset is one of the reasons of slow execution of the algorithms. It is not advisable to reduce number of records from a dataset since they may contain useful information. However, number of features in a dataset can be reduced.

There are two main ways to reduce features in a dataset:

1. Correlated features can be merged resulting in lesser number of features.
2. Choose features that cause maximum variance in the dataset as well as in the output.

The second method is normally preferred and several statistical techniques have been developed in this regard e.g. Factor Analysis, Linear Discriminant Analysis (LDA) and Principal Component Analysis (PCA). In this chapter we will study PCA and in the next chapter we will study LDA.

## *Principal Component Analysis Theory*

Principal component analysis is one of the most widely used techniques for dimensionality reduction. PCA works by selecting features that cause maximum variance in the output, leaving behind features that have no effect on the output. The intuition behind this approach is that variance can be used as a measure for distinguishing output; hence features that are responsible for distinguishing outputs are more important and hence should be selected. First principal component is the feature that results in maximum variance, similarly second principal component is the feature that causes second largest variance and so on.

PCA has two major advantages:

1. Reduced number of features means reduced training time, thus faster execution time.
2. We can only view data in three dimensions; in higher dimensions it is not particularly easy to view the data. With reduced number of features, data can easily be viewed.

It is important to mention here that data must be scaled before applying PCA since variance can be huge for features expressed in higher units such as kilograms, millions, light years etc. Therefore, PCA can be biased towards features these features.

## *Implementing PCA with Sklearn*

In this section, we will see how we can use Python's Scikit Learn library to implement principal component analysis. Using PCA, we will find the most important features from the bank note authentication data. We have four attributes in the dataset i.e. entropy, skewness, variance and curtosis of the wavelet transformed image of the currency note.

More details about the dataset can be found at this link.

The dataset has been supplied with the book and can be found by the name of banknote_data.csv in the Datasets folder. Follow these steps

### 1- Importing Required Libraries

```
import pandas as pd
import numpy as np
import matplotlib.pyplot as plt
%matplotlib inline
```

### 2- Importing the Dataset

The following script imports the dataset.

```
banknote_data = pd.read_csv(r'D:\Datasets\banknote_data.csv')
```

The script above reads the dataset and stores it in *banknote_data dataframe*.

### 3- Analyzing the Data

The following script returns the data dimensions:

```
banknote_data.shape
```

The above script returns (1372, 5) which means that our dataset contains 1372 records and five attributes.

To see how the data looks like, execute the following script. It returns the first five rows of the data.

```
banknote_data.head()
```

The output looks like this:

|   | Variance | Skewness | Curtosis | Entropy | Class |
|---|----------|----------|----------|---------|-------|
| 0 | 3.62160  | 8.6661   | -2.8073  | -0.44699 | 0 |
| 1 | 4.54590  | 8.1674   | -2.4586  | -1.46210 | 0 |
| 2 | 3.86600  | -2.6383  | 1.9242   | 0.10645 | 0 |
| 3 | 3.45660  | 9.5228   | -4.0112  | -3.59440 | 0 |
| 4 | 0.32924  | -4.4552  | 4.5718   | -0.98880 | 0 |

### 4- Data Preprocessing

To following script divides the data into feature and label set.

```
features= banknote_data.iloc[:,0:4].values
labels= banknote_data.iloc[:,4].values
```

Finally let's divide the data into 80 % training and 20% test sets:

```python
from sklearn.model_selection import train_test_split
train_features, test_features, train_labels, test_labels = train_test_split(features, labels, test_size = 0.2, random_state = 0)
```

### 5- Scaling the Data

For Random Forest algorithm, it is not necessary to scale the data, however just for the sake of practice, let's scale the data using standard scalar. Remember we discussed scaling in the 3rd chapter.

```python
from sklearn.preprocessing import StandardScaler
feature_scaler = StandardScaler()
train_features = feature_scaler.fit_transform(train_features)
test_features = feature_scaler.transform(test_features)
```

## 6- Applying PCA

It is very easy to implement PCA via sklearn library, we need to use PCA class of the *sklearn.decomposition* library. The number of principal components to select can be passed as parameter to the PCA class. If no number of components is passed, all the features are selected as principal component. Next, we need to call the fit and transform methods and pass them the training and test features. We do not need to pass the output since PCA is an unsupervised learning technique and calculates variance from the feature set alone. Execute the following script to get all the four principal components for the banknote_data.csv dataset.

```
from sklearn.decomposition
import PCA


pca = PCA()
train_features =
pca.fit_transform(train_featu
res)
```

```
test_features =
pca.transform(test_features)
```

Now, to see the variance retrieved by each component sorted by descending order, print the *explained_variance_ratio_* attribute on the screen as shown below:

```
exp_var =
pca.explained_variance_ratio_
print(exp_var)
```

The output looks like this:

```
[ 0.54159993  0.32604745  0.08719788  0.04515474]
```

From the output, it can be seen that the first principal component is responsible for 54.15 % variance in the dataset, similarly the second principal component causes 32.60 percent variance in the dataset.

## Performance Evaluation with One Principal Component

Let's evaluate how the Random Forest algorithm performs with only one principal component. Repeat the steps 1 to 5 (Not step 6) in the previous section and then execute the following script:

```
pca = PCA(1)
train_features = pca.fit_transform(train_features)
test_features = pca.transform(test_features)
```

Now let's train Random Forest algorithm on train features with one principal component and test the algorithm on test features. Execute the following script:

```
from sklearn.ensemble import RandomForestClassifier

rf_clf = RandomForestClassifier(n_estimators=50, random_state=0)
rf_clf.fit(train_features, train_labels)
predictions = rf_clf .predict( test_features)
```

Finally let's see how well the Random Forest algorithm performs with one principal component. Execute the following script:

```
from sklearn.metrics import classification_report, confusion_matrix, accuracy_score
print(confusion_matrix(test_labels, predictions))
print(classification_report(test_labels, predictions))
print(accuracy_score(test_labels, predictions))
```

The output looks like this:

```
[[101  56]
 [ 42  76]]
             precision    recall  f1-score   support

          0       0.71      0.64      0.67       157
          1       0.58      0.64      0.61       118

avg / total       0.65      0.64      0.65       275

0.643636363636
```

With one principal component, the accuracy achieved is 64.36%.

## Performance Evaluation with Two Principal Component

To evaluate, performance with 2 principle components, execute the following script:

```
pca = PCA(2)
train_features = pca.fit_transform(train_features)
test_features = pca.transform(test_features)
from sklearn.ensemble import RandomForestClassifier

rf_clf = RandomForestClassifier(n_estimators=50, random_state=0)
rf_clf.fit(train_features, train_labels)
predictions = rf_clf.predict( test_features)
```

Finally let's see how well the Random Forest algorithm performs with two principal components. Execute the following script:

```
from sklearn.metrics import classification_report,
```

```
confusion_matrix,
accuracy_score
print(confusion_matrix(test_l
abels, predictions))
print(classification_report(t
est_labels, predictions))
print(accuracy_score(test_lab
els, predictions))
```

The output looks like this:

```
[[145  12]
 [ 22  96]]
              precision    recall  f1-score   support

           0       0.87      0.92      0.90       157
           1       0.89      0.81      0.85       118

avg / total       0.88      0.88      0.88       275

0.876363636364
```

With two principal components, the accuracy achieved is 87.63%. Similarly, with three and four components the accuracy improves to 98.54% and 99.63%. This shows that the accuracy improvement diminishes after 3 components; therefore 3 components can be retained.

### Conclusion

In this chapter, we saw how we can use PCA for dimensionality reduction. In the next chapter, we will see how we can use LDA for dimensionality reduction. Happy Coding!

## *Chapter 17*

## *Dimensionality Reduction with LDA*

In the previous chapter, we saw how what dimensionality reduction is and how we can use Principal Component Analysis (PCA) to reduce number of features in a dataset. In this chapter we will see how we can use LDA for the same purpose.

## *Linear Discriminant Analysis Theory*

LDA is a supervised dimensionality reduction technique which tries to select features based on their ability to distinguish the output. LDA relies on the output of the records as well. Where as in PCA, feature set is enough and labels are not required for feature reduction. As a first step in LDA, related data points are clustered together before being projected into a new dimension where the distance between each cluster is maximized. Similarly, the distance between each data points and its corresponding cluster centroid is minimized.

## *Implementing LDA with Scikit Learn*

In this section we will implement LDA with Python's Scikit Learn library. We will again try to reduce dimensions of the banknote_data.csv dataset. Follow these steps:

### 1- Importing Required Libraries

```
import pandas as pd
import numpy as np
import matplotlib.pyplot as plt
%matplotlib inline
```

### 2- Importing the Dataset

The following script imports the dataset.

```
banknote_data = pd.read_csv(r'D:\Datasets\banknote_data.csv')
```

The script above reads the dataset and stores it in *banknote_data dataframe*.

### 3- Analyzing the Data

The following script returns the data dimensions:

```
banknote_data.shape
```

The above script returns (1372, 5) which means that our dataset contains 1372 records and five attributes.

To see how the data looks like, execute the following script. It returns the first five rows of the data.

```
banknote_data.head()
```

The output looks like this:

|   | Variance | Skewness | Curtosis | Entropy | Class |
|---|----------|----------|----------|---------|-------|
| 0 | 3.62160  | 8.6661   | -2.8073  | -0.44699 | 0 |
| 1 | 4.54590  | 8.1674   | -2.4586  | -1.46210 | 0 |
| 2 | 3.86600  | -2.6383  | 1.9242   | 0.10645  | 0 |
| 3 | 3.45660  | 9.5228   | -4.0112  | -3.59440 | 0 |
| 4 | 0.32924  | -4.4552  | 4.5718   | -0.98880 | 0 |

### 4- Data Preprocessing

To following script divides the data into feature and label set.

```
features=
banknote_data.iloc[:,0:4].val
ues

labels=
banknote_data.iloc[:,4].value
s
```

Finally let's divide the data into 80 % training and 20% test sets:

```
from sklearn.model_selection
import train_test_split

train_features,
test_features, train_labels,
test_labels =
train_test_split(features,
labels, test_size = 0.2,
random_state = 0)
```

### 5- Scaling the Data

For Random Forest algorithm, it is not necessary to scale the data, however just for the sake of practice, let's scale the data using standard scalar. Remember we discussed scaling in the 3rd chapter.

```
from sklearn.preprocessing
import StandardScaler
```

```
feature_scaler =
StandardScaler()
train_features =
feature_scaler.fit_transform(
train_features)
test_features =
feature_scaler.transform(test
_features)
```

### 6- Applying PCA

It is very easy to implement PCA via sklearn library, we need to use *LinearDiscriminantAnalysis* class of the *sklearn.discriminant_analysis* library. The *n_components* parameter is used to set the number of linear discriminants. Next, we need to call the fit and transform methods and pass them the training features and training labels. Remember in case of PCA we only needed to pass the feature set and not the labels. Execute the following script to get the first linear discriminant for the dataset.

```
from
sklearn.discriminant_analysis
```

```
import LinearDiscriminantAnalysis


LDA = LinearDiscriminantAnalysis(n_components=1)
train_features = LDA.fit_transform(train_features, train_labels)
test_features = LDA.transform(test_features)
```

## Performance Evaluation with One Linear Discriminant

Now let's train Random Forest algorithm on train features with one linear discriminant and test the algorithm on test features. Execute the following script:

```
from sklearn.ensemble import RandomForestClassifier


rf_clf = RandomForestClassifier(n_estimators=50, random_state=0)
```

```
rf_clf.fit(train_features,
train_labels)
predictions = rf_clf
.predict( test_features)
```

Finally let's see how well the Random Forest algorithm performs with linear discriminant. Execute the following script:

```
from sklearn.metrics import
classification_report,
confusion_matrix,
accuracy_score
print(confusion_matrix(test_l
abels, predictions))
print(classification_report(t
est_labels, predictions))
print(accuracy_score(test_lab
els, predictions))
```

The output looks like this:

```
[[156   1]
 [  1 117]]
             precision    recall  f1-score   support

          0       0.99      0.99      0.99       157
          1       0.99      0.99      0.99       118

avg / total       0.99      0.99      0.99       275

0.992727272727
```

Here accuracy achieved with 1 linear discriminant i.e. 99.27% is compared to 99.63% achieved by four principal components in last chapter.

**Conclusion**

In this chapter, we studied LDA in detail. If the data is uniformly distributed LDA will outperform PCA in most cases. However in case of irregular data, PCA performs better. Furthermore PCA can be used with labeled as well as unlabeled data. Happy Coding!!!

# Chapter 18

## Performance Evaluation with Cross Validation and Grid Search

Welcome to the final chapter of the book. In this chapter we are going to see how we can evaluate performance of an algorithm in a more robust way.

Till now we have been evaluating algorithm performance using by splitting the data into training and test sets and then training the model on the training set and testing it on the test set. However there are certain problems associated with this approach. One such problem is variance. This problem can be solved using Cross Validation.

Another problem that affects the performance comparison of different algorithms is use of various hyper parameters such as K in KNN algorithm and n_estimators in Random Forest algorithm.

To compare two algorithms, we need to find the parameters that result in best performance. This problem can be solved using Grid Search algorithm.

In this chapter, we will study Cross Validation and Grid Search in detail.

## *Cross Validation*

Earlier we said that splitting data randomly into training and test set can lead to variance problem. Variance in performance evaluation of an algorithm refers to scenario where an algorithm performance varies depending upon the test set being used.

Cross validation is the solution to variance problem. In cross validation, dataset is divided into K folds where K is any integer. Each of the K folds or partition is at least once used in the training set as well as testing set. For instance let's divide the dataset into 5 partitions. In the first iteration, first 4 partitions are used for training and $5^{th}$ partition is used as testing.

In the second fold, 1,2,3 and 5$^{th}$ partition is used for training and 4$^{th}$ partition is used for testing. In this way every partition is used at least once for testing. The final performance of the algorithm can be evaluated by taking mean of the results from individual tests. This solves variance problem since now the result is based on algorithm being trained and tested on the complete dataset.

## *Cross Validation with Python's Scikit Learn*

The problem that we are going to solve with Random Forest algorithm cross validation is predicting the quality of wine depending upon several features.

More details about the dataset can be found at this link. We will only use the dataset for the red wine. Data has been supplied with the book and can be found in the Datasets folder with name redwine_data.csv.

Follow these steps

## 7- Importing Required Libraries

```
import pandas as pd
import numpy as np
import matplotlib.pyplot as plt
%matplotlib inline
```

## 8- Importing the Dataset

The following script imports the dataset.

```
redwine_data = pd.read_csv(r'D:\Datasets\redwine_data.csv', sep=';')
```

The script above reads the dataset and stores it in *banknote_data dataframe*.

## 9- Data Analysis

To see how the data looks like, execute the following script. It returns the first five rows of the data.

```
redwine_data.head()
```

The output looks like this:

| | fixed acidity | volatile acidity | citric acid | residual sugar | chlorides | free sulfur dioxide | total sulfur dioxide | density | pH | sulphates | alcohol | quality |
|---|---|---|---|---|---|---|---|---|---|---|---|---|
| 0 | 7.4 | 0.70 | 0.00 | 1.9 | 0.076 | 11.0 | 34.0 | 0.9978 | 3.51 | 0.56 | 9.4 | 5 |
| 1 | 7.8 | 0.88 | 0.00 | 2.6 | 0.098 | 25.0 | 67.0 | 0.9968 | 3.20 | 0.68 | 9.8 | 5 |
| 2 | 7.8 | 0.76 | 0.04 | 2.3 | 0.092 | 15.0 | 54.0 | 0.9970 | 3.26 | 0.65 | 9.8 | 5 |
| 3 | 11.2 | 0.28 | 0.56 | 1.9 | 0.075 | 17.0 | 60.0 | 0.9980 | 3.16 | 0.58 | 9.8 | 6 |
| 4 | 7.4 | 0.70 | 0.00 | 1.9 | 0.076 | 11.0 | 34.0 | 0.9978 | 3.51 | 0.56 | 9.4 | 5 |

## 10- Data Preprocessing

The following script divides the data into feature and label set.

```
features=
redwine_data.iloc[:,0:11].val
ues
labels=
redwine_data.iloc[:,11].value
s
```

Since we will be using cross validation and it will automatically be splitting the data into training and test set, here using train_test_split we will a lot all the data to training_features and set test size to zero by passing zero to test size variable as shown below:

```
from sklearn.model_selection
import train_test_split
train_features,
test_features, train_labels,
test_labels =
train_test_split(features,
```

```
labels, test_size = 0,
random_state = 0)
```

## 11- Scaling the Data

For Random Forest algorithm, it is not necessary to scale the data, however just for the sake of practice, let's scale the data using standard scalar. Remember we discussed scaling in the 3rd chapter. We will only scale train_features since there is no data in the test_features variable.

```
from sklearn.preprocessing import StandardScaler
feature_scaler = StandardScaler()
train_features = feature_scaler.fit_transform(train_features)
```

## 12- Cross Validation

To apply cross validation, the first step is to choose the algorithm that you want to use for cross validation. The following script initializes Random Forest classifier with 500 estimators.

```
from sklearn.ensemble import RandomForestClassifier
rf_clf = RandomForestClassifier(n_estimators=500, random_state=0)
```

To apply cross validation, the *cross_val_score* class of the *sklearn.model_selection* library is used. The classifier, feature set and label set and the number of folds for cross validation are passed as parameter to the *cross_val_score* class as shown below:

```
from sklearn.model_selection import cross_val_score
rf_accuracies = cross_val_score(estimator=rf_clf, X=train_features, y =train_labels, cv=5)
```

In the script above, we perform 5 fold cross validation.

To see the accuracies returned by the *cross_val_score* class for all the five folds, you can print the list of values returned by *the cross_val_score* class as follows:

```
print(rf_accuracies)
```

The above script returns following results:

```
[ 0.7173913   0.68224299  0.71028037  0.68867925  0.69085174]
```

You can see that accuracies of all the five folds are more or less similar.

To see the average of all the accuracies, you can call mean() function on the list as shown below:

```
print(rf_accuracies.mean())
```

The result shows: 0.69788 i.e. 69.788%.

Finally to see the standard deviation, execute the following script:

```
print(rf_accuracies.std())
```

The above script returns 0.0135 or 1.35% which is very less. Therefore we can say that our dataset has very less variance and results obtained on all the sets are can be considered correct and close to the average.

## *Gird Search for Parameter Selection*

Job of a machine learning algorithm is to find best set of parameters or weights that yield best results. These parameters are found by the algorithms and depend upon the dataset. We cannot control these parameters.

However there is another set of parameters that is specified before the algorithm is run. For instance value of K for the KNN algorithm, the type of kernel for the SVM algorithm, the number of estimators for the Random forest algorithm, number of nodes for the neural network and so on. These parameters can be controlled or specified.

However we do not really know the best value for these parameters. In the last section we set the n_estimator for the Random Forest algorithm to 500. However we do not know if this is the ideal. What if the algorithm performs better with 200 or 700 nodes? OR what is the best value of K? 10 Or 20? We do not know the answer to these questions.

Grid Search algorithm helps us solve this problem. Basically what Grid Search algorithm does is, it automatically finds best parameters for a particular algorithm from a set of parameters.

## *Implementing Grid Search with Sklearn*

The Python's Scikit Learn library comes with a package to implement Grid Search. For this purpose the sklearn.model_selection class contains GridSearchCV class that can be used to implement Grid Search. However before that some preprocessing is required.

### Creating Parameter Dictionary

Grid search algorithm doesn't just randomly run and finds all the best parameters for an algorithm because it can take years. For instance if grid search algorithm starts testing each value for the number of estimators parameter from 1 to 1000, the algorithm has to run a minimum of 1000 times and that's just for 1 parameter. Therefore a set of values for each parameter that you want to test, is passed to the GridSearchCV class. These set of parameters and are expressed in the form of a dictionary.

Suppose we want to test different values for n_estimators, warm_start and criterion parameters of the Random Forest algorithm, we can create a dictionary that looks like this:

```
param = {
    'n_estimators': [100, 250, 500, 750, 1000],
    'warm_start': ['True', 'False'],
    'criterion': ['entropy', 'gini']
}
```

In the script above we create a dictionary named, "param" the keys for the dictionary are the names of the parameters and the values of the dictionary corresponds to values of the parameter. From these set of values, the Grid Search algorithm will return the best combination.

For instance we want to test the best value for n_estimators parameter and we passed 100, 250, 500, 750 and 1000. Grid search will select best value from these five values. It is important to mention here that grid search algorithm can take lot of time depending upon the values that you want to test and the number of folds for the cross validation.

For instance in our case we have 5 values for n_estimators parameter, 2 values for warm_start and two values for criterion. Total possible combinations in this case are 5 x 2 x 2 = 20. Multiply this value with number of folds e.g 5. That makes it 100 executions. This can slow down the algorithm a bit.

## Creating Parameter Dictionary

To execute the Grid Search, we need create object of GridSearchCV class and pass it the classifier (we will use Random Forest classifier created in the last section), the parameter dictionary that we just created, the performance evaluation metrics (we will use accuracy), cross validation folds and the number of jobs. When n_jobs = -1, it means that all the CPU's should be used for performing Grid Search. Execute the following script to create GridSearch object.

```
from sklearn.model_selection import GridSearchCV
grid_search = GridSearchCV(estimator=rf_clf,
param_grid=param,
scoring='accuracy',
                cv=5,
                n_jobs=-1)
```

The final step is to call fit method on the GridSearchCV object and pass it the training and test set as shown below:

```
grid_search.fit(train_features, train_labels)
```

This can take a bit of time to execute.

Once the above script executes, the last and final step is to see the parameters selected by grid search, to do so you can use the best_params_ attribute of the GridSearchCV class as shown below:

```
optimal_parameters = grid_search.best_params_
print(optimal_parameters)
```

The output looks like this:

```
{'criterion': 'gini', 'n_estimators': 750, 'warm_start': 'True'}
```

Best achieved with aforementioned parameters values. Finally to see the accuracy achieved using most optimal parameters, execute the following script:

```
optimal_results = grid_search.best_score_
```

```
print(optimal_results)
```

## Conclusion

With this chapter, this book comes to its end. From here on I would suggest you to study machine learning on your own. Following are some of the very good resources:

1. For Python: https://www.python.org/
2. For Machine Learning: http://scikit-learn.org/stable/
3. For Deep Learning: https://keras.io/
4. For datasets: https://archive.ics.uci.edu/ml/index.php

*You Might Also Be Interested In...*

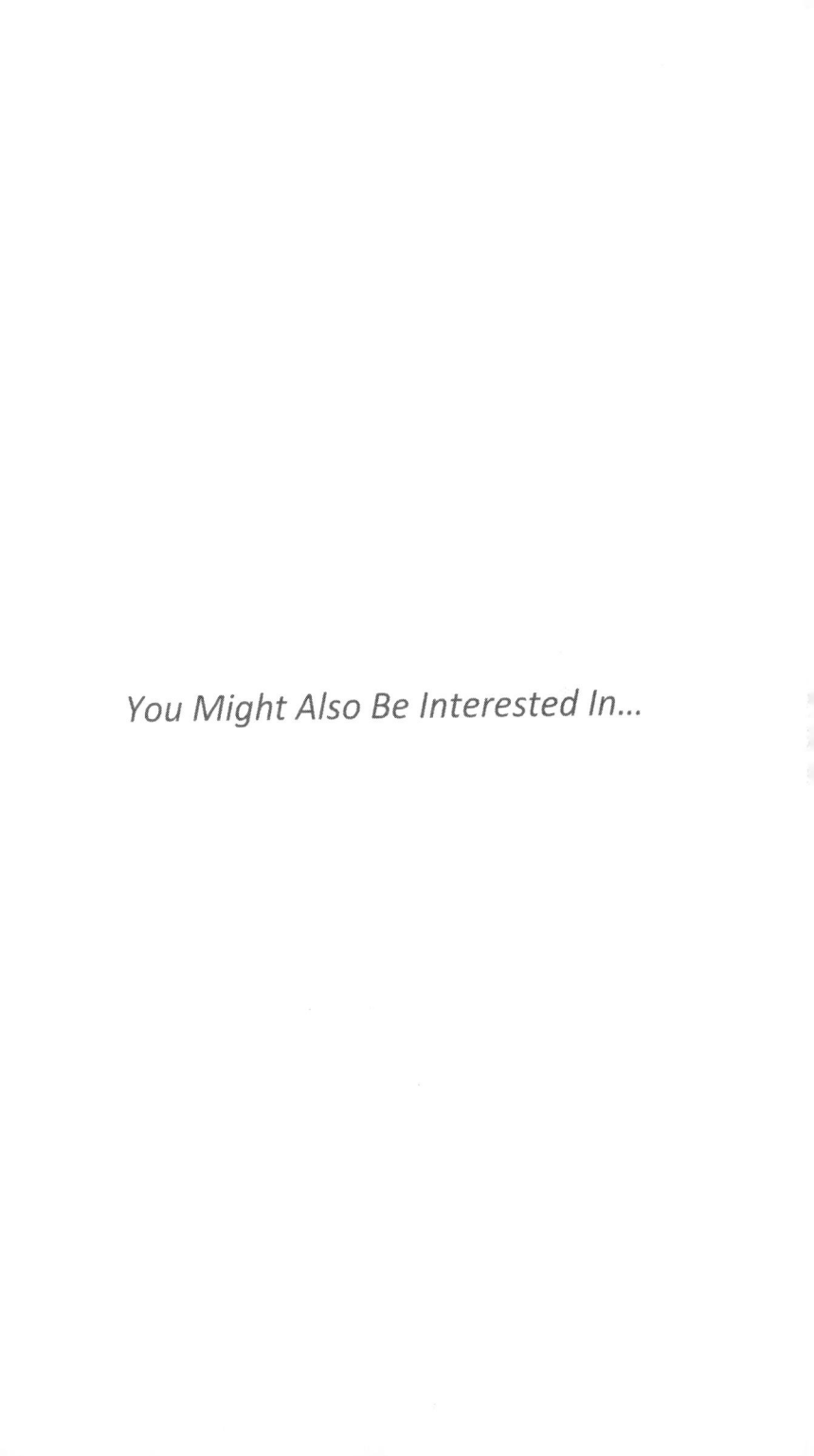

**Book Link:** *https://amzn.to/2AiwYHf*

## DATA ANALYTICS GUIDE FOR BEGINNERS
### INTRODUCTION

William Sullivan

*FREE E-BOOK DOWNLOAD :*

http://bit.ly/2yJsyq4

or

http://pragmaticsolutionstech.com/

Use the link above to get instant access to the bestselling E-Book **Data Analytics' Guide For Beginners**

Printed in Great Britain
by Amazon